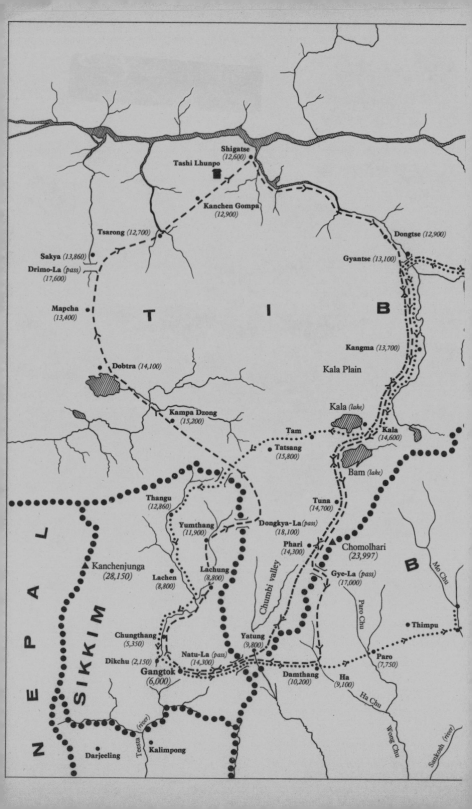

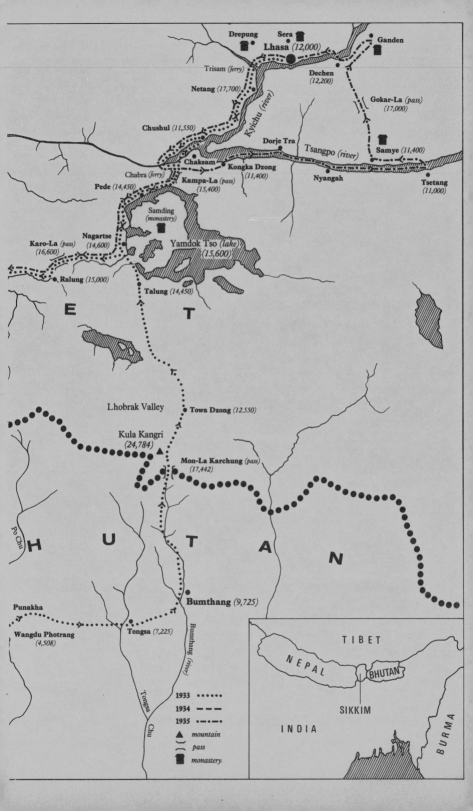

Drepung Sera Ganden
Lhasa *(12,000)*
Trisam *(jerry)* Dechen
(12,200)
Netang *(17,700)* Gokar-La *(pass)*
(17,000)
Chushul *(11,550)* Kyichu *(river)*
Dorje Tra Tsangpo *(river)* Samye *(11,400)*
Chabra *(jerry)* Chaksam Kongka Dzong Nyangah Tsetang
Pede *(14,450)* *(11,400)* *(11,000)*
Kampa-La *(pass)*
(15,400)
Samding
(monastery)
Nagartse Yamdok Tso *(lake)*
Karo-La *(pass)* *(14,600)* *(15,600)*
(16,600)
Ralung *(15,000)* Talung *(14,450)*

E T

Lhobrak Valley Towa Dzong *(12.550)*

Kula Kangri
(24,784)
Mon-La Karchung *(pass)*
(17,442)

Po Chu H U T A N

Bumthang *(9,725)*

Punakha
Wangdu Photrang Tongsa *(7,225)* Bumthang *(river)*
(4,508)

Tongsa
Chu

1933 ....
1934 - - - - -
1935 -·-·-·-

▲ *mountain*
) (*pass*
🏛 *monastery*

TIBET
NEPAL BHUTAN
SIKKIM
INDIA BURMA

Memoirs of a Political Officer's Wife
in Tibet, Sikkim and Bhutan

Memoirs of a Political Officer's Wife in Tibet, Sikkim and Bhutan

Margaret D. Williamson

Written in collaboration with John Snelling
Foreword by Dzasa Jigme Taring

Wisdom Publications · London

First published in 1987.

Wisdom Publications, 23 Dering Street, London W1,
England.

British Library Cataloguing in Publication Data
Williamson, Margaret D.
    Memoirs of a political officer's wife in Tibet,
    Sikkim and Bhutan.
    1. South Asia—Politics and government
    I. Title II. Snelling, John, *1943* –
    954   DS341
ISBN 0 86171 056 8

Set in Garamond 11 on 13 point by Setrite of Hong
Kong, and printed and bound by Valentine Sands of
Melbourne, Australia, on 80 gsm cream Sunningdale
Opaque paper supplied by Link Publishing Papers of
West Byfleet, Surrey.

Contents

Foreword

I AM VERY happy to know that Peggy Williamson has written an autobiography in collaboration with John Snelling. It is both an honour and a pleasure for me to have been asked to contribute this Foreword, for Peggy has been an intimate friend of my wife, Mary, and myself since the time of her first visit to Tibet, as was her husband, Derrick, until his premature death in 1935.

I feel that any book concerned with Tibet before the Chinese Invasion of 1950 is not only of general interest but has historical and educational significance as well. A large number of books about Tibet have in fact appeared, but one such as this, written by someone who was not only a true friend of the Tibetan people but also officially concerned with the foreign affairs of Tibet, is a rare and precious document indeed. It gives a true picture of the free and rich culture that existed in Tibet during the time of the Thirteenth Dalai Lama, with whom the author was privileged to have an audience just a few weeks before his death in 1933.

Peggy's husband, Derrick Williamson, was a man of wide knowledge and experience in the field of foreign service, particularly in the Himalayan and Central Asian regions. He was gifted with a gentle and adaptable character that enabled him to deal most efficiently with official matters. As such he was admirably suited to take charge of relations between British India and her northern neighbours: Sikkim, Bhutan and Tibet. During his time as Political Officer in Sikkim, he made it his business to be on good terms with the various officials with whom he had to deal, including those in Tibet, by whom he was loved as a true friend rather than merely an official visitor. We were therefore deeply saddened by his tragic death.

His wife, Peggy, our dear friend, was also most efficient and caring in carrying out her duties as the wife of a senior British official and this no doubt contributed in no small measure to the success of her husband's work in cementing friendly relations between our two countries. Peggy was very popular among the ladies of Tibet and to her is furthermore due the credit for organizing the first ladies' party, with guests drawn from different tiers of society. She also gave the first children's party ever held in Lhasa, an event that was throughly enjoyed by all those who attended it.

Mary and I , both of whom treasure such happy memories of her, would like to offer our warm congratulations to Peggy for having here set down the record of her experiences.

Jigme Taring
Rajpur, India
1987

Acknowledgements

FOR MANY YEARS I have dreamed of writing a book that would be a fitting memorial to Derrick's work and our life together in Tibet, Sikkim and Bhutan. That this has finally been achieved is due to the help and kindness of many friends.

I am deeply grateful to my neighbour and friend Betty Scott, and to her late husband Dr Gordon Scott, who gave so much valuable advice and assistance over many years. I especially thank Nicholas Rhodes, who not only provided the spark that encouraged me to start the book, but also gave many precious hours to ensure that it became a reality.

To my many Himalayan friends go warm thanks for friendship extending over more than fifty years. My sincere thanks go to Jigme Taring, who with his wife, Mary-la, were my closest friends in Tibet.

I offer my thanks to the Royal Family of Bhutan for the warmth of their friendship, particularly Rani Chuni Dorji, Ashi Tashi Dorji and Her Majesty Ashi Kesang Wangchuck, Queen Mother of Bhutan. My thanks are extended to the Sikkim Royal Family for their kind friendship.

I thank John Snelling for augmenting the material in my original diaries and papers with material from the archives of the India Office Library and elsewhere, and for lending his literary skills to the drafting of the narrative. Finally, I should like to thank Robina Courtin and her colleagues at Wisdom Publications for publishing my memoirs.

Introduction: The Land of the Gods

THERE HAS ALWAYS been something mystically compelling about the Himalayas. They stretch magnificently across the full extent of India's northern horizon, a monolithic bulwark of foothills, above which appear the soaring snow peaks themselves. So high, cool, remote and peerlessly white, they catch and return the ever-changing light of the sun with redoubled radiance. There among the dazzling snows and mighty glaciers rise the great rivers that bring water and life to the sultry plains. There too, high above the noise and bustle of the world, holy men and women retreat in search of the solitude and silence in which one may encounter the infinite and the eternal. It is indeed a land of the gods.

FIFTY YEARS AGO, when the British ruled an Empire in India, their power extended into the Himalayas and beyond. Much of the western Himalayas fell under the administration of the British Raj, and although the various kingdoms occupying the central and eastern Himalayas enjoyed a greater or lesser degree of independence, British influence was never entirely absent. In the eastern Himalayas, for instance, a Political Officer—a member of an official service created by the Bristish to serve in the native states and in areas beyond the frontiers—was resident in Gangtok, the tiny capital of the equally tiny state of Sikkim. The PO Sikkim was also responsible for official dealings with the considerably larger eastern Himalayan state of Bhutan, and with Tibet, that vast and mysterious land often called the 'Roof of the World' lying as it does on a high and remote plateau beyond the main Himalayan crestline.

A fortuitous combination of circumstances enabled me, from comparatively humdrum beginnings in the north of England, to live and travel in Sikkim, Bhutan and Tibet during the heyday of the British Raj. I was able to move freely in all circles in those countries, from the humblest to the most exalted and, with only one or two minor exceptions, to see whatever I wanted to see. Thus I was able to gain unique insight into many aspects of three remarkable societies. I shall always count myself highly privileged for this, particularly as in many places extensive upheavals have taken place with the result that so much of what I saw fifty years ago has now sadly gone for ever.

SANDWICHED BETWEEN Bhutan and Nepal, Sikkim occupies an area of some 2,800 square miles on the southern slopes of the eastern Himalayas. It is situated due north of the Bay of Bengal, with no intervening high ground, and so is subject to the highest rainfall of any part of the Himalayan range during the period of the summer monsoon. As a result, the flora is varied and spectacular, ranging from subtropical in the deep valleys that lie only a few hundred feet above sea level to alpine in the vicinity of the great peaks of Kanchenjunga, which, at over 28,000 feet, is the third highest mountain in the world. Over 4,000 species of flowering plants have been recorded, including more than 450 species of orchid and forty varieties of rhododendron. Seven hundred bird species have also been recorded and over 600 types of butterfly—a remarkable range for such a small area.

The indigenous inhabitants of Sikkim are the Lepchas, a small, shy, gentle people, said to love animals, plants and music. They speak a Tibeto-Burmese language and their religion is Buddhism. In the early sixteenth century, the ancestors of the ruling family of Sikkim migrated from the province of Kham in eastern Tibet and settled in the Chumbi valley, a low-lying wedge of Tibetan territory penetrating southwards across the main Himalayan crestline and neatly dividing northern Sikkim from northern Bhutan. The ruling family had little difficulty establishing its power over the Lepchas to establish a kingdom in Sikkim, though relations between the two races were not always harmonious. Greater threats to the territorial integrity of the kingdom were posed by the Nepalese and the Bhutanese, however, both of whom made incursions into Sikkimese territory, particularly in the eighteenth century. It was in fact the British who finally drove the Nepalese out of south-western Sikkim during the Anglo-Nepalese War of 1814–15. Thereafter the boundary between Sikkim and Nepal was established by the Treaty of Titalya (1817), with Britain agreeing to arbitrate in any dispute between the two parties.

Thus the Sikkimese became involved with the British in India and, within a decade, British mediation was sought over the matter of some Lepchas who had fled from Sikkim and sought refuge in Nepal. Not long after this a certain Captain Lloyd managed to persuade the Sikkimese to cede the virtually uninhabited Darjeeling Ridge for use by the British as a hill sanatorium. Over the years, however, Darjeeling grew and prospered with the result that the Sikkimese felt that the wiley Westerners had tricked them out of a valuable piece of their territory. Relations were strained for a while and matters eventually came to a head when the Sikkimese forcibly detained the famous botanist Sir Joseph Hooker. Military action ensued, followed in 1861 by a treaty. This recognized Sikkimese authority but at the same time confirmed the annexation of the whole of the Darjeeling district.

This treaty brought Sikkim fully into the British sphere of influence, and during the reign of Sidkeong Namgyal (1863–74) relations improved. Sidkeong was succeeded by the fourteen-year-old Thutob Namgyal, under whom misunderstanding arose again. The young Maharaja was bitterly opposed to the policy of allowing Nepalese immigrants to settle in Sikkim, a policy vigorously supported both by some of his own Sikkimese-Tibetan subjects who stood to gain financially, as well as by the British who could see advantages in having the land developed by vigorous Nepalis.

The Maharaja, however, failed to stop large-scale immigration and consequently, deeply frustrated, he withdrew to spend the greater part of his time on his estates in the Chumbi Valley. He also tried unsuccessfully to mediate in certain border disputes that arose between the British and the Tibetans in the 1880s. Increasingly dissatisfied with the situation in Sikkim, the British now intervened and appointed John Claude White to be the first Political Officer, resident in Gangtok and with a brief to reorganize the administration of the state. This he did, creating a state council but retaining a great deal of power in his own hands, with the result that difficulties arose in the relationship between White and the Maharaja. These persisted until full administrative powers were handed over to Thutob Namgyal in 1905. Responsibility was then allocated among several ministers and a secretariat was set up. Thereafter, the British Political Officer in normal circumstances merely acted as an adviser, although he did retain a right of veto.

Thutob Namgyal died early in 1914 and was succeeded by his son, Sidkeong Namgyal, a highly intelligent young man, who, in addition to a traditional Sikkimese monastic education, also benefited from two years spent at Oxford University. Unfortunately, Sidkeong did not live to fulfil his potential, dying prematurely after less than a year in office. He was succeeded by his younger brother, Tashi Namgyal.

In 1918 Sikkim was granted full internal autonomy. The Political Officer continued in residence, however, and although in theory he merely acted in an advisory capacity in the sphere of internal affairs, in practice his presence in Gangtok meant that he continued to enjoy considerable influence. As regards external affairs, these were controlled by the Government of India through the Political Officer.

BHUTAN, ON THE OTHER HAND, is an independent Buddhist kingdom comprising some 18,000 square miles and with a population of about one million. As it has remained more closed and isolated from outside influences than any of the other Himalayan kingdoms, it has managed to develop a unique form of Tibetan culture admirably adapted to its lush forests, mountainous terrain and seasonally wet climate.

The population of Bhutan is of three main types. In the high valleys of western and central Bhutan one finds people of Tibetan ancestry, who made their way into the country from the ninth century onwards. In the east, the people are of a generally similar ethnic type and may in fact be the original inhabitants of the land. In the south, on the other hand, an increasing number of Nepalese immigrants have, over the last century, begun to settle the steep, forested valleys.

Having such a low population density, the Bhutanese tend to enjoy a rather higher standard of living than their neighbours. Each family grows enough food to satisfy its own needs and lives a largely self-sufficient life. The people take great pride in weaving the beautifully patterned cloth out of which their clothing is made. The national sport is archery and the Bhutanese people devote a lot of time to it.

The low population has also meant that the wildlife of Bhutan has not been driven from its natural habitat as has happened in so many other parts of the world. The flora is also as varied as the fauna, but both have been little studied due to the small number of foreign visitors. All in all, Bhutan is a naturalist's paradise.

We know very little of the history of Bhutan prior to 1600. Each valley seems to have enjoyed a largely self-sufficient existence with little or no political unity. Certain valleys, however, definitely benefited from the trans-Himalayan trade as two of the easiest passes across the snow mountains lead through Bhutan.

Modern Bhutanese history properly begins with the arrival in the early seventeenth century of Shabdung Ngawang Namgyal, a religious leader of the Drugpa school of Tibetan Buddhism. He travelled south from Tibet with his followers and set up a Buddhist state in Bhutan, with a code of laws and a system of government that was to remain unchanged for 250 years. He built *dzongs* (fortresses) all over the country and these served both as monasteries and as seats of administration, as well as fulfilling a defensive purpose. As in the case of the Dalai Lamas of Tibet, the Shabdung was both the religious and the secular leader of the country. The lineage was passed down through reincarnations and when a Shabdung died his new incarnation would be sought. Often indications would be given as to where to search for the incarnation; perhaps moss might suddenly grow on the side of a pillar, indicating the direction for the search, or an oracle might have a vision giving other clues. Once a child was found who might be the new Shabdung, he would be tested and if he passed the tests he would be recognized as the incarnation of the previous Shabdung. Unfortunately, after the first, few Shabdungs – also known as Dharma Rajas – survived to maturity, with the result that the reins of government were usually in the hands of a succession of Regents or Deb Rajas. Each Regent was elected by and ruled through a State Council consisting of ten of the most powerful local chieftains, each of whom held feudalistic sway in a particular area. This system of government proved to have an inherent weakness, however, in so far as it endowed the local chieftains with an excess of power. Thus, although in theory the State Council elected the Deb Raja to rule the country, in practice the most powerful chieftain or Penlop was able to ensure that a puppet nominee was elected. Even the few Dharma Rajas that attained maturity were not able to rule as the first Shabdung had done. The result of this was that Bhutan was torn by almost continuous civil war as the various local chieftains vied for superiority.

Relations between the Bhutanese and the British in India were not always good and the two powers actually fought minor wars in 1772 and 1865. These deprived the Bhutanese of the flat, fertile territories that they once occupied to the south of their native hills, but the British never extended hostilities into the hills themselves, nor did they seek to influence the course of Bhutanese politics. Bhutan thus always enjoyed complete independence from the British, unlike its neighbour, Sikkim.

During the 1880s, the Tongsa Penlop, Ugyen Wangchuk, emerged as the most powerful chieftain and during the next forty years was to have a greater influence upon the running of his country than anyone since the first Shabdung. In 1903 the reigning Shabdung passed away and no successor could be found. Eventually it was decided that the most advantageous course for the future would be to do away with the posts of Dharma and Deb Raja, to strengthen the central government and to elect a king. Thus in 1907 Ugyen Wangchuk became the first hereditary King of Bhutan.

The new king continued to rule through the State Council (or Council of Ministers) but the power of the local chieftains was greatly reduced and in consequence the country at last enjoyed peace. In the sphere of foreign policy, Ugyen Wangchuk recognized the advantages that would accrue from friendly relations with British India. To this end he acted as mediator between the British and the Tibetans during the Younghusband affair of 1904 and paid a personal visit to Calcutta in 1906. The visit did a tremendous amount towards cementing friendly relations between Britain and Bhutan. Claude White, the PO Sikkim, was invited to be present at the coronation of Ugyen Wangchuk in 1907, and in 1910 a treaty was signed whereby, in exchange for agreeing to be guided by the British Government in foreign affairs, the Bhutanese secured an undertaking that the British would not attempt to exercise any control over the internal affairs of their country.

Liaison between the British and Bhutanese governments was maintained through the good offices of the PO Sikkim and Raja Ugyen Dorji (and subsequently his son, Raja Sonam Tobgye Dorji), who resided for part of each year in Kalimpong. The Political Officer made very occasional tours of Bhutan but, apart from him and his entourage, Europeans were permitted to travel in the country only in the most exceptional circumstances, with the result that Bhutan managed to remain almost completely free of twentieth-century influences. It was indeed only in 1960, some twenty-seven years after my own first visit there, that the first road was built.

Ugyen Wangchuk died in 1926 to be succeeded by his son, Jigme Wangchuk, and the country has enjoyed the able rule of the Wangchuk family ever since.

MORE THAN EITHER SIKKIM OR BHUTAN, Tibet has exercised a particular fascination over the Western mind and until very recently it was something of a 'Forbidden Land,' entry into which was strictly prohibited for all but the privileged few. This exclusiveness allowed a unique and spiritually rich culture to blossom on the Roof of the World and to survive, virtually untouched by the rest of the world, until about thirty years ago when Tibet was taken over by the Chinese Communists. Since then it has continued to be a closed country, though for different reasons. In the last few years, however, entry regulations have at last been relaxed and Westeners have been able to visit Tibet more freely than ever before. Sadly, what visitors bring away with them are reports of the dreadful destruction wreaked by the Communists upon the old culture that they supplanted by force of arms.

Tibet is a vast country comprising some 500,000 square miles, much of it at altitudes in excess of 13,000 feet above sea level. This, added to the fact that it is bounded on nearly all sides by formidable mountain ranges, endows it with a natural seclusion additional to its man-made one. China, which has presently swallowed up Tibet, lies to the north and east, India to the south.

Of the major regions of Tibet, the notorious Chang Tang or Great Northern Plain is a vast area of inhospitable deserts, snow-capped mountain ranges and salt lakes, subject to some of the worst inclemencies of climate and temperature. When I travelled in Tibet, it was virtually uninhabited except for a handful of tough nomads who migrated there to graze their flocks during the summer months and then re-treated before the onset of the terrible winter. Occasionally these nomads augmented their subsistence living with a little banditry.

Eastern Tibet, on the other hand, which in past centuries simply blurred into the Celestial Empire of China, is chopped by the upper reaches of three great rivers: the Yangtse, the Mekong and the Salween. Here lies the province of Kham, home of the Khampa, traditionally the most martial and lawless of the Tibetan peoples.

Finally there is southern Tibet which, though largely arid and hilly, contains numerous fertile valleys where barley and other crops can be grown to support relatively substantial settled communities. Naturally it was here that the bulk of the population lived and where the major towns are situated: Shigatse, Gyantse and the capital, Lhasa. Besides these towns there were just scattered villages and hamlets – and vast empty spaces. Fifty years ago, the population of this huge land, equal in area to half the size of Europe, probably did not exceed 3,000,000.

ONE ELEMENT IN TIBETAN LIFE I noticed during my visits was the central importance of Buddhism, which originated in India and was brought to Tibet during the seventh century AD. Until that time the Tibetans were reputed to have been a warlike people, but the teachings of Buddha transformed them.

Everywhere you went in Tibet fifty years ago you came across evidence of religion. A sizeable proportion of the population lived in monasteries and nunneries, and the lay people of all classes were very religious. At spare moments during the day people turned prayer-wheels or murmured mantras. Every house had a shrine or shrine-room, prayer-flags fluttered upon every roof and even the wayside rocks were carved with Buddhist mantras or images. Pilgrimage was popular too, and the year was sprinkled with important festivals, many of which had a religious character.

Buddhism lays special emphasis on the virtues of patience,

acceptance and loving-kindness. It also extols not harming others, for if one regards one's own suffering as an unwanted burden, it follows that all beings feel likewise. One should therefore refrain from any action that might cause harm to any sentient being, human or otherwise.

A central concept in Buddhism is reincarnation, where a person's mental continuum incarnates not just once, but many times. Those who have gained mastery over their mind can control their rebirth, unlike most sentient beings who are projected relentlessly into countless rebirths. Where it is considered beneficial, a lama may reincarnate in a recognized lineage. One example of this is His Holiness the Dalai Lama, whose lineage dates back to the fourteenth century. (The present Dalai Lama, the fourteenth, now lives in exile in northern India, where his function as both the spiritual and the temporal leader of Tibet is carried out.) The Government is headed by His Holiness—when I was in Tibet it was Thubten Gyatso, the Thirteenth Dalai Lama—and below him are one or more Prime Ministers or *Lönchen*, a Cabinet or *Kashag* composed of four or more *Shapés* and a National Assembly. The latter, in which all strata of Tibetan society are represented, used to debate issues of the day. It was here in particular that the great monasteries gave voice to their opinions and were a powerful influence in the land. It was monastic opinion that maintained a check upon all attempts to introduce any form of 'progress' into Tibet.

It is often charged that the old Tibet was an essentially feudal society. This cannot be denied. Aside from the religious, there were only two classes: the peasantry and the aristocracy—though latterly a middle class was just beginning to emerge.

The aristocracy, whose privileges were numerous, shared administrative power with the religious and many posts were in fact split between a lay and a monk incumbent. The special status of high officials was carefully emphasized in various ways: the way they did their hair as well as the robes and jewellery they wore all denoted rank in some way. There was also a special honorific language that it was important to use when addressing high-ranking people.

In old Tibet there were the invisible inequalities and abuses found in all societies, but one never came across that restiveness and resentment so common in the West. There was also little crime. Indeed, what endures most powerfully in my mind after fifty years is how happy the Tibetans were. Their land may have been arid and unproductive; they may have lacked modern conveniences; their climate was at times exceedingly harsh; their social system was undemocratic and their system of administration open to abuse – yet in spirit they were always resilient and joyful. They had deep faith in their religion, and loved to enjoy themselves at picnics, parties and festivities; and once you had a friend among them, you had a friend for life.

RELATIONS BETWEEN TIBET AND THE BRITISH in India may be traced back to the late eighteenth century when the East India Company sent two of its servants on missions there, primarily with a view to opening up trading connections. Both the amiable Scot, George Bogle (1775), and Captain Samuel Turner who followed him (1782), got as far as the great monastic complex at Tashilhunpo, the seat of the Panchen Lama near Shigatse in southern Tibet, but neither was allowed to go to Lhasa, the only place where their business could have been effectively concluded. It was not until 1811 in fact that an Englishman at last succeeded in reaching the holy city. This was Thomas Manning, Sinophile and friend of Charles Lamb. How a solitary and unaccredited traveller managed to succeed where the best efforts of official ones had failed remains something of a mystery. Perhaps Manning's very eccentricity worked in his favour. However, although he met the youthful Dalai Lama of the day, his sojourn in Lhasa was a miserable affair made all the more so by paranoid fantasies of imminent arrest and execution. 'Dirt, dirt, grease, smoke. Misery but good mutton' – such was Manning's verdict on Tibet.

Manning was the great exception. No other British traveller reached Lhasa during the nineteenth century. Indeed,
following the Gurkha Wars of 1788—92, when armies from
Nepal twice overran southern Tibet, a curtain of exclusiveness came down and for more than a century Tibet remained
the 'Forbidden Land' from which all Western travellers were
strictly debarred. This, of course, did not deter the stout-
hearted from attempting to enter Tibet, but such people
invariably travelled furtively, at great personal risk and none
succeeded in reaching Lhasa.

Having for long pursued a policy described by Sir Francis
Younghusband as one of 'drift and inaction', towards the end
of the nineteenth century the British began to make efforts
to put their relations with their northerly neighbour on a
more regular footing. The Tibetans, however, no doubt
encouraged by their Chinese suzerains, stubbornly refused to
deal with the British and the century ended with a series of
vexing and apparently insoluble border disputes.

Then, while the Tibetans were spurning British overtures
and returning official letters unopened, rumour reached the
ears of the Viceroy of India, Lord Curzon, that the Dalai
Lama was communicating with the Russian Tsar via a sinister
Buryat lama named Dorjiev. This precipitated the Younghusband Expedition of 1903—04, when a British army
actually forced its way deep inside Tibetan territory and
eventually occupied the capital itself. The Tibetans, now no
longer able to avoid talking, eventually came to terms and in
the absence of the Dalai Lama, the Great Thirteenth, who
had fled to Mongolia, a treaty was negotiated with his Regent
and signed with all due pomp in one of the great halls of the
Potala, the imposing winter palace of the Dalai Lama in
Lhasa.

Among other things, this treaty granted the British the
right to set up trade agencies in southern Tibet, so that for
the first half of this century there were British officials
actually present on Tibetan soil, notably at Yatung and
Gyantse.

One might have thought that the Younghusband affair would have permanently soured Anglo-Tibetan relations. Not so, however. In 1910, when a Chinese army invaded Tibet and took the capital, the Dalai Lama again fled, not to Mongolia as before, but to British India. There he lived in exile in Darjeeling for nearly two years and made a firm friendship with Charles Bell, then PO Sikkim. This friendship continued after His Holiness returned to his capital in 1913, the Chinese having in the interim been soundly trounced and evicted. During the First World War His Holiness offered the British 1,000 Tibetan troops and special prayers were performed for the success of the British military effort. Then in 1920, Bell was able to pay a long official visit to Lhasa to see his old friend. Some sections of Tibetan society were rather anti-British at that period but, by the time he left, Bell had been able to convince one and all with consummate diplomatic skill that he was a true friend of the Tibetan people.

DURING THE LATTER PART OF HIS REIGN, the Great Thirteenth Dalai Lama was intent upon securing his country's independence from the Chinese, with whom his country had had a long and often difficult relationship. After his exile in India, he was aware that to do this he would have to introduce some measure of modernization into Tibet and, especially, establish at least the semblance of an up-to-date military capability. He looked very much to British India for help in this and received limited supplies of arms and military training for some of his troops. The telegraph line that the Younghusband Expedition had taken as far as Gyantse was extended to Lhasa with British help, thus for the first time placing the Tibetan capital in contact with the outside world. Perhaps more surprising, however, was the fact that four Tibetan boys—Ringang, Kyipup, Gongkar and Mondö, a monk—were sent to Rugby School to receive an English education. Ringang subsequently received training in electrical engineering too. In 1923 a school run upon

English lines was set up in Gyantse under the headmaster-
ship of Frank Ludlow, but, frowned upon by the monks, it
unfortunately enjoyed only a brief life.

Charles Bell was followed as Political Officer by Colonel
F.M. (Eric) Bailey, who in 1924 spent four weeks in Lhasa.
Bailey was one of the great Central Asian travellers and
explorers, and, like Bell, spoke fluent Tibetan. When he
reached Lhasa in 1924, Bailey found Tibetan officials very
disturbed by the flight of the Panchen Lama from Tibet the
year before. There had for a long time been rivalry between
the administrations of the two senior Lamas of Tibet, and
the Chinese had in fact encouraged this as a way of
undermining the power of the Lhasa Government. Things
came to a head in the early twenties when Lhasa tried to
reassert its authority over its honoured vassal, in particular
insisting that he pay a contribution towards the cost of the
new army. Appeals were made to the British Government
for mediation but were refused on the grounds that the
British did not want to become involved in Tibet's internal
affairs. In 1923, the Panchen Lama departed in despair, first
for Mongolia and then went on to China. These events led
the Tibetans to doubt the benefits of friendship with the
British and for several years no invitation was extended to the
Political Officer to visit Lhasa.

In 1929 however, relations between Tibet and Nepal
reached a crisis on account of the seizure of a fugitive from
the Nepalese Embassy in Lhasa. Both countries had mobil-
ized their armies and the British were concerned lest war
break out. To avert this danger, a special envoy, Sardar
Bahadur Laden La of Darjeeling, was sent to Lhasa to
mediate. The Dalai Lama was persuaded to take a concili-
atory line and tension was defused.

Developing a fresh appreciation of the advantages of British
friendship from this incident, the Dalai Lama sent an invitation to Bailey's successor as PO Sikkim, Colonel Leslie
Weir, to visit Lhasa. No easy resolution was available to the
ongoing problem of the fugitive Panchen Lama, however.

The Tibetan Government was now more eager than ever to secure his return for it feared that he might be manipulated by the Chinese and used as a pretext for future aggression. The major stumbling-block was the fact that the Panchen Lama had specified unacceptable terms for his return. When Colonel Weir left Lhasa at the end of November 1932, the Dalai Lama's parting request was that the British should act as mediators in any future negotiations with the Chinese.

While Colonel Weir was in Lhasa, my future husband, Derrick Williamson, deputized for him in Gangtok, and knew that at the end of that year he would take over as Political Officer in Sikkim, Bhutan and Tibet. This was the world in which I was to find myself in the spring of 1933.

1 My Early Life

I was born in 1906 of Scottish lowland stock, although I was brought up in the Wilmslow district of Cheshire. We were a large and happy family of six boys and three girls: I was the seventh child.

Something of a tomboy, I had a special passion for animals and learnt to ride well at an early age. This was to stand me in good stead in the years ahead. Knowing that I loved animals an Irish lady friend made me a special offer one day, when I was nine years old.

'Peggy,' she said. 'I'm too old to use our donkey, Jenny, any more. Please use her yourself as if she were your own.' I was delighted and took her at her word. This was during the First World War and there was a hospital for war wounded quite near us. I had a half holiday from school on Wednesday afternoons and that gave me a bright idea.

'I could take two soldiers out for a drive in the donkey cart,' I said to my mother, 'that is, if Jenny will go!'

Jenny was a rather contrary creature; I'm afraid that with her it was always a matter of 'sometimes she will, sometimes she won't.'

'Well, I suppose, yes,' Mother replied after a moment's reflection; 'but, of course, you'll have to ask the Matron up at the hospital first.'

So it was that I, a small girl full of good intentions, found myself making my way nervously to the Matron's office. I was more than a little overawed, but behind that well-starched apron she must have had a kind heart for she did give me her permission and sent me off with a warm smile.

The rides were a great success. After the first session, the men actually began to queue up for me and there were often far more than I could take. Jenny behaved herself passably well, though she was always eager to return home. There were often occasions when we rounded the last corner on one wheel of the donkey cart!

There is a sequel to this little episode. In November 1918, James, who worked in the telegraph section of the local post office, and who used to phone my brothers on Saturday nights to give them the results of football or cricket matches, came to see me.

'They're having a great procession in the village to celebrate the Armistice,' he informed me; then added, 'they'd like you and Jenny to be in it.'

I gasped with surprise. 'Oh, I couldn't do that!'

'Don't you worry about anything,' James reassured me. 'I'll polish up her hooves and tack, and I'll lead her.'

James's offer gave me confidence. 'All right, then,' I conceded. 'But we'd better go at the back of the procession.'

And that is what we did, and Jenny behaved beautifully. James came up with a splendid banner with PEACE emblazoned on it for me to hold and the donkey cart was trimmed with laurel leaves, much to the amusement of my family.

MY FATHER, JAMES MARSHALL, was a businessman dealing in fabrics and he often travelled abroad for Glasgow firms, who eventually moved him south to Manchester. A good linguist, he spoke several languages. He apparently spoke Spanish with a marked Scottish accent!

My first contact with the Mysterious East came about through an uncle of my mother who had worked for Jardine Matheson in Hangkow. He shared a house near Lockerbie in Dumfriesshire with his brother and two sisters in which my mother was brought up, a house I visited many times during my childhood. I remember clearly all the fascinating oriental objects that Uncle William Dobie had brought back with him from China.

When I was fifteen I was sent away to boarding school, to Brentwood in Southport, following in the footsteps of my two elder sisters. However, a turnabout in the family fortunes, a trauma for all concerned, meant that my education had to be cut short after about a year, my father having lost a large portion of his capital. Nevertheless, the family rallied and bore the misfortune well. Most of my brothers and sisters were by now married and no longer an expense for my parents.

Although I had to abandon my education, as yet incomplete, I wasn't prepared to waste my time kicking my heels at home. I borrowed £50 from my mother, took the best secretarial course I could find and determined to earn my own living as soon as I could. Jobs were not easy to come by in the economically uncertain twenties but to my great satisfaction and even before I had completed the secretarial course, I managed to land myself an excellent position with the Madge Atkinson and Mollie Suffield School of Dancing in Manchester. I earned the princely sum of £2.10s for a five and a half day week.

In 1932, however, an unexpected holiday in the west of England was to set in train a series of events which changed my life. That hastily arranged trip to Torquay would result in my being spirited away from my home in the north of England and set on the trail of the court of the Dalai Lama of Tibet and the little-known kingdoms of Bhutan and Sikkim.

IN 1932, FREDERICK WILLIAMSON of the Foreign and Political Department of the Government of India, then Acting Political Officer in Sikkim, came home to England on leave. My family had known the Williamsons—also of Lowland Scottish stock—for many years, and Frederick, who was also known as Derrick, usually made his home with his uncle and aunt, Rupert and Dorothy Williamson of Bury in Lancashire, when he was in this country. On this, his fourth home leave, however, another uncle had generously placed at his disposal a fine modern house at Torquay. Meeting Derrick's aunt by chance one day, I got all the news about his visit from her.

'I must get down to see him,' she told me. 'Unfortunately, I'll have to take the train – and long train journeys are so tedious.'

Half jokingly, I replied: 'Oh, don't bother with the train. I'll drive you down in the car.'

To my surprise she accepted and as I had Whit Week off there was no problem with making arrangements for the office.

I had seen quite a lot of Derrick Williamson in the past. He had come to visit us on numerous occasions, although as he was fifteen years older than me and I was having a very good time at home, I didn't take these visits particularly seriously.

On this occasion, however, things took an entirely different turn. Once we got to Torquay, Derrick and I found ourselves drawn together. We were so obviously happier in each other's company than in anyone else's that the others took note and gave us time to be together. We walked, we just sat, and we talked endlessly. Derrick of course had many tales of all the places to which he had been posted in the East, and the places that he had visited on leave, and I listened with fascination. He had such love and enthusiasm for the people and lands in which he had worked, especially for Sikkim, Bhutan and Tibet, that it was difficult not to be captivated.

We were sitting talking about the Himalayas one evening as the sun set with fiery magnificence into the western ocean when Derrick paused and asked me if I would like to come out to Sikkim the following year. Taken aback, I could think of nothing to say, but after a moment's thought I said that I would love to.

Nothing more was said at the time: there certainly wasn't a definite proposal of marriage. However, during the following months after Derrick had returned to his post in Sikkim, letters postmarked in the East began to reach me in increasing numbers. The matter of my possibly going out was raised again and became a reality. For me there was never any dilemma: I knew that I wanted to go. Finally, it was agreed that I should do so in the spring of 1933.

But first, two major hurdles had to be surmounted: my parents had to be told and their permission gained, and then I had to get enough money to pay for my passage.

My mother proved to be no problem. When I explained the situation to her, she merely smiled knowingly, and said: 'I thought something like that was afoot.' She was entirely understanding.

My father, however, was an altogether different proposition. Some twenty years older than my mother, he was very much the Victorian patriarch and I approached him with some trepidation. However, after I had summoned all my courage he listened carefully to everything I had to say and then reacted quite differently to what I had expected. He just sat in his chair, silently reflecting upon the matter.

'Well,' he said eventually, 'it's your life. But if things don't work out for you and Derrick, always remember that there's a place for you at home here with your family.'

I was overjoyed and thought that, for a very Victorian father, it was a most marvellous thing for him to say. We left it that when I got out to Derrick, I would cable home to say whether I was staying or whether I would be coming home.

The financial aspect turned out to be a knottier problem. There was certainly no hope of my saving up the necessary sum from my modest wages, and of course I could not ask my parents for assistance as they had financial problems of their own. There was one other way, though. My mother had been brought up by two aunts, Aunt Mary and Aunt Maggie, after whom my eldest sister and I had been named. Now Aunt Mary had left sister Mary £500 and so Mary was in a position to lend me the £250 that I needed – which she offered to do when I explained the situation to her. I for my part felt free to accept her kind offer because I knew that whatever Aunt Mary did for her Aunt Maggie would certainly do for me, so sooner or later I should be able to pay Mary back. It was gambling, I admit—but gambling on a certainty.

So I was able to pay for my ticket and also had a small amount left over to buy the few things that I needed to take with me. My sisters and my closest friends rallied round and helped me make my trousseau by holding afternoon sewing parties. After we'd finished, I had just about everything—bar a wedding dress. To take one out would be tempting Providence, I thought.

My eldest brother, Jim, the brother I was always closest to, got me a berth on a ship sailing from Liverpool to Calcutta and at last the day dawned when I was to be away. All the Williamsons and all the Marshalls came to see me off from the quay. It was at the same time a very happy and a very sad occasion. The two families did everything for my comfort. On 4 March 1933, I set sail for the East.

*The Great Thangka at
Gyantse.*

Derrick in Tibetan dress.

*Gyantse Town,
showing the great
Chörten, the Polkhor
Choide.*

Derrick with Chinese officials at Aksu, June 1929.

Frank Ludlow at Mt. Kailas.

My brother Bill Marshall with Derrick and Mr & Mrs Mira Gyalwa (Tibetan Trade Agent at Yatung) and Norbhu, August 1931.

Derrick filming at Kashgar.

With the Consulate staff at Kashgar.

(Opposite) Hunting eagle at Kashgar.

The Residency, Gangtok.

Interior of the Residency.

Kanchenjunga from the Residency ; Gangtok Bazaar.

(Opposite) Wedding group. Top row: Maharaja of Sikkim, Rani Dorji, self and Derrick, Maharani of Sikkim, Raja Dorji and Dr Graham. Middle row: Kula, Tashi-la and Coocoo-la; the Toplis children, George-la and Jean-la and George Sherriff.

Self with Bess and
Robert Toplis and
Bruce.

Ashi, head-mali.

Lugi.

The Anderson Bridge over
the Tista on the road up to
Gangtok.

2 Frederick Williamson

DERRICK WILLIAMSON BELONGED to that rare and happy breed who are lucky enough to find their true vocation in life. He found his life's fulfilment working as a Political Officer among the Buddhist peoples of Sikkim, Bhutan and Tibet.

As for his early life, this was rather cosmopolitan. Born on 31 January 1891 in Bury, Lancashire, he was the eldest child of Arthur and Emma Williamson, and had a brother, Toby, and a sister Bess. One of his early memories was of all the family going up to London from Essex, where they were then living, to watch the celebrations for Queen Victoria's Diamond Jubilee in 1897. Later that year Arthur Williamson was posted to Australia by his employers, the Western Electric Company, to set up the first telephone exchange there.

The whole family travelled to Australia together, sailing first to New York on the newest P & O ship, the *Coronia*. Everything on that great ship was upholstered in red and the corridors and companionways were vast. Derrick never got lost in them, however; he had an excellent sense of direction, even as a child. After New York, they crossed the North American continent by rail and then sailed on to Australia by way of Honolulu.

On arriving in Australia, the Williamsons set up house at Mosman, a suburb of Sydney. Derrick and his brother Toby went to North Shore Grammar School; they had great fun crossing Sydney Harbour every day by ferry. At school

Derrick displayed an early flair for languages, winning a scholarship chiefly on account of his prowess in French, to the amazement of his family and friends. Afterwards he never missed an opportunity to learn new languages, a propensity which proved invaluable in his later career in the Indian Political Service. He also took music lessons and likewise never lost his early love for music.

In 1899, tragedy struck the young family when their beloved mother, Emma, died prematurely. Derrick was just eight years old. Their father moved the family to a bungalow just outside Sydney to live with his friends, Mr. and Mrs. Prickman, where they were to spend four happy years.

In 1903 the Williamsons sailed home to England on the oldest P & O ship, the *Victoria*, then making her final voyage before being sent to the breakers' yard. The *Victoria* had sails as well as propellers. On their return to England, they went to the family home in Nottingham, where they lived for a time with their grandparents and numerous unmarried uncles and aunts. Derrick's over-solicitous grandmother would not let them use carving knives or even scissors—in marked contrast to the free and easy and adventurous life they had enjoyed in Australia, where Derrick and Toby used to go heaving a long-handled axe out in the bush to bring home barrowloads of logs for the winter fire.

Derrick continued to be a promising scholar and eventually won a scholarship to Bedford Modern School; Toby went with him as well. They joined Mr. Allen's house, also known as 'Kipper's House' after Mr. Allen's nickname. As well as being an enthusiastic oarsman, Derrick distinguished himself academically at school and won Mr. Allen's accolade as 'the best brain that has passed through my hands'. He won no less than thirteen prizes, one of which, awarded for good work in the sixth form, was Archibald Williams's *The Romance of Modern Exploration*. This recounted the thrilling adventures of intrepid explorers in little-known parts of the world. Interestingly, one of the illustrations depicted the Potala, the great winter palace of the Dalai Lama of Tibet in

Lhasa. 'This is probably the only photographic view of the palace in existence,' the caption claimed. The text, meanwhile, contained accounts of the Tibetan adventures of the great Swedish explorer, Sven Hedin, and also those of the Englishman, Captain Deasy. Perhaps the stories in this beautiful leather-bound book, embossed with the school crest, sowed in Derrick's impressionable mind the seeds of an interest in those remote parts of the world.

Derrick went on to Cambridge in 1909, winning a scholarship to Emmanuel College. He read mathematics and was classed senior optime in the 1912 Tripos. Being a keen oarsman, he stroked the Lent Boat in his first year, the second May Boat in his second year and the first Lent Boat in his final year. He was a fellow NCO with Robert Gardner in the Emmanuel Company (D) of the Cambridge University Officers' Training Corps, in which he rose to the rank of colour sergeant. Mr. Gardner remembered him at the time as being 'spare and slightly built, and in temperament very conscientious'. He might also have added thrifty, for to save the train fare from Chingford in Essex, where the family home was by then situated, to Cambridge, Derrick used to bicycle the whole way, sleeping out under hedges if darkness fell while he was still upon the open road.

ON COMING DOWN FROM CAMBRIDGE, Derrick went to Wrens, the well-known Indian Civil Service coaching establishment. He passed his ICS examinations in 1913 and arrived in India the following year. His first posting was to Dhanbad in Orissa, where he made friends with a Mr. and Mrs. Mackie. Mr. Mackie, who managed a coalmine for Mackinnon Mackenzie, was a great polo player and he instilled a love of the game in Derrick.

When the Great War broke out on 4 August 1914, Derrick very much wanted to join up but was initially deterred from doing so by the Government of India. Eventually, however, they sent him a telegram, which he received just as he was setting off for the recruiting centre in Dhanbad. Realizing intuitively what its message was, he just stuffed it into his pocket and did not read it until he reached his destination.

He had wished to join the Gurkhas, but was sent first of all to the Middlesex Regiment in Palestine. On 4 October 1916, he had his wish fulfilled when he was transferred to the 1st King George V's Own Gurkha Rifles, then serving in Mesopotamia (modern Iraq). He served with the battalion both there and in Palestine until 1st June 1918, when he was transferred along with the rest of his Company to the newly-raised 4/11th Gurkha Rifles.

Derrick distinguished himself in the war during the Battle of Jabal Hamin. On 25 March 1917, both Colonel Dopping-Heppenstall and Captain Northey being wounded, he was the senior remaining officer and commanded the battalion until Major Evans returned from sick leave in India to take over command. Derrick was himself wounded on the east side of Kut East Mounds and was mentioned in dispatches.

After the war, Derrick enjoyed a period of leave and then returned to India. He was posted to the Chapra district of Bihar as Personal Assistant to Frank Luce, the Magistrate and District Officer. There, besides work and finding himself a proficient teacher to give him lessons in Persian, he also found time for tennis with the local planters. That appointment lasted a year; afterwards, in 1920, Derrick saw service on the North-West Frontier as Assistant Commissioner at Charsadda. While he was there someone told him about wonderful jobs with the Foreign and Political Department. Thinking that these might provide just the openings and opportunities for which he was looking, he decided to apply.

The Political Service was entirely separate from the Indian Civil Service. Of it, Sir Basil Gould, Derrick's immediate successor as PO Sikkim, has written:

> This Service, of which the Viceroy was the Head, was concerned with most of the self-governing States, which extended over a third of the area of India and accounted for a quarter of the country's

population; with the North-West Frontier Province and Baluchistan; and with areas beyond the frontiers of India such as Aden, the Persian Gulf, parts of Persia, Afghanistan, Nepal, Bhutan and Tibet. Its personnel of about 150 officers was recruited approximately two-thirds from the Indian Army and one-third from the Indian Civil Service. Although the Department was known in my early days as the Foreign Department and later as the Foreign and Political Department, and later still was divided into two departments, External and Political, we were always known as Politicals (from *The Jewel in the Lotus* by B.J. Gould, London, 1957).

'To a jealous outside world, "a Political" might be a term of abuse,' Gould concluded. 'To us it was a term of glory.'

Such a service offered unique attractions to men with an adventurous turn of mind. There was the chance to live and work 'beyond the frontiers' and get to know little-known peoples, to travel along unfrequented byways, to explore and enjoy the thrills of *shikar* (the Hindu word for sport, especially hunting and shooting). Furthermore, being posted well away from the main centres of administration meant that there was the possibility of enjoying a high degree of independence.

Derrick's acceptance into the Political Service was not immediate, however. In 1912, still with the ICS, he was posted to Mysore as Secretary to the Resident; and in 1923 he spent eleven months in Hyderabad in a similar capacity, working largely on matters to do with the visit of the Viceroy.

It was while he was enjoying his first stint of leave in 1922 that Derrick learnt that his application to join the Political Service had been successful. His first posting was to Tibet as British Trade Agent (BTA) in joint charge of the two important agencies at Gyantse and Yatung. Normally each had its own Agent, but at times, as in this case, the two posts were combined. The posting, which lasted from 1924 until 1926, also meant that Derrick was Assistant to the Political Officer in Sikkim, Colonel Eric Bailey.

The Agency at Gyantse had been set up under the terms of the Treaty signed by Colonel Younghusband in Lhasa in 1904. Younghusband's own Secretary, the Tibetan-speaking Captain Frederick O'Connor became the first BTA and was popular with the Tibetans because of his generous nature and attractive personality. He also startled them considerably when he imported a two-seater "Baby Peugeot" motor car across the Himalayas and proceeded to drive it about the Plain of Tuna at a ferocious 15 mph! O'Connor's successors at Gyantse included Colonel Leslie Weir, B. J. Gould, Major W. L. Campbell and David Macdonald, an official of mixed Scottish and Sikkimese extraction who also held the Yatung post for many years.

The BTA Gyantse was provided with an Escort of Indian Troops commanded by either one or two British officers. A Warrant Officer of the Supply and Transport Corps of the Indian Army was in charge of the Commissariat Department, while two British military telegraphists were responsible for postal and telegraphic communications. The Head Clerk also tended to be an ex-military man. Finally there was a Medical Officer and his assistants; Derrick was fortunate to have the services of good men like Rai Sahib Bo, a Sikkimese surgeon attached to the Indian Medical Service (IMS).

The Agency at Yatung, being situated in the pleasantly wooded Chumbi Valley and not therefore on the Tibetan plateau proper, was not subject to the worst rigours of the Tibetan climate. Gyantse was, however, and life at the Agency there was blighted in winter by regular dust-storms and bitter cold. From November until March, the double windows at the Agency were sealed and all the personnel donned heavy furs, lambswool underclothing and Gilgit boots. Christmas was a keenly anticipated respite, but for the festivities everything had to be hauled up from India over the Himalayas: the turkey, the fruit and even the beer, which of necessity had to be thawed out because it invariably arrived frozen solid. Relief was found in games. Football, hockey and tennis were played, and there was even a polo ground. The Tibetans were also prepared to turn a blind eye to shikar—as long as it was pursued well away from religious establishments.

For men billeted together under such conditions from one year's end to the next with hardly any society other than their own, things could inevitably become more than a little trying. Of course, for anyone equipped with the right temperament, it was an ideal life and there were indeed those who sought to spin out their tours of duty in Gyantse as long as possible. For most, however, the privations and the narrowness of the life were difficult to bear, and the altitude—Gyantse is situated at over 13,000—was an additional aggravation. Inevitably pressures built up and nerves became frayed. Some resorted to bizarre practical jokes as a way of letting off steam; a few snapped—like Johnson, the Head Clerk, who in 1917 blew his brains out. He was buried in the little cemetery shared jointly there by Christians and Moslems after 1904, and the local Tibetans used to swear that on dark nights they saw him sitting astride the wall, calling out to passers-by for cigarettes. This story itself may well have arisen from a practical joke played by one of the Agency personnel!

Derrick was one of that minority who instantly fell under the spell of Tibet, a fascination which was to last for the remainder of his life. Following in the footsteps of his great predecessor, Sir Charles Bell, he set himself to learn the language and also studied the local folklore, customs and religion. He was always sympathetic to Tibetan Buddhism and, fully appreciating what was good in it, dismissed the contentions of those who saw it as base superstition. This deep and lasting love of Tibet was later extended to embrace the Himalayan kingdoms of Sikkim and Bhutan, and he was prepared to forgo promotion and other career prospects in order to remain working among their peoples.

DERRICK LEFT THE DUAL POST of BTA Gyantse and Yatung

on 31 May 1926. He was for a time in 1926–7 Officiating Political Officer in Sikkim. Then, in 1927, he went on leave for a second time and travelled in Australia, New Zealand and China.

While in China Derrick was able, with the full permission of the Government of India, to visit the Panchen Lama in the small monastery in which he was then living at Mukden. The Panchen Lama fled Tibet late in 1923, just a short while before Derrick received his first posting there, but the reverberations of this event were still echoing through the land. During the interview, which took place on 28 February, Derrick told His Serenity that he came in a purely private capacity but that if there was anything that he could do to help him, he would be pleased to oblige. The Panchen Lama thanked him and said that he had sent a message both to the Government of India and to the Dalai Lama to the effect that he had left Tibet 'entirely owing to my own fault' and that he proposed to return as soon as possible. Derrick got him to repeat this to make sure that he had heard it correctly. Further to that His Serenity had no definite plans, but he and Derrick discussed various routes by which he might eventually return to Tibet, Derrick favouring one by sea via British India rather than an overland one, which would take him through areas 'tainted with Bolshevism'.

The Panchen Lama's manner through the interview was cordial but somewhat nervous. They were never alone for long and, as the room in which they were meeting was just a temporary structure with matting walls, there was always the danger of being overheard by eavesdroppers. For this reason the more confidential parts of their conversation were spoken in whispers. Derrick felt that His Serenity looked older than might have been expected and quite ill. Indeed, he did admit that the intense cold of Mukden had lately been troubling him. One souvenir of this historic meeting that remains in my possession is the fine photographic portrait that the Panchen Lama gave to Derrick, signed and sealed in the best Tibetan manner.

HAVING ALSO MANAGED to fit in six weeks at home in England during this leave, Derrick returned to the East to find himself posted as Consul-General to Kashgar, the most westerly of the string of oasis towns dotted along the Old Silk Road in the arid wastes of eastern Turkestan (Chinese Sinkiang, as it is known today). Situated far to the north of Kashmir and accessible only after long and gruelling treks along tortuous mountain trails through the Karakoram or the Pamir, Kashgar was an out-of-the-way posting by any standards. 'The isolation is extreme,' wrote Sir Eric Teichman, the notable British consular official who went there in 1935. 'I can recall no other British Consulate which is, in time and difficulties of travel, so far away.'

When Derrick arrived in Kashgar on 27 October 1927, he found his Vice-Consul, George Sherriff, had been there holding the fort since August. George was a most genial young man. The son of a Scotch whisky distilling house, he was trained as a professional soldier at Woolwich and eventually commissioned. While in the Army, he was looked upon as an outstanding young officer, and his sociable ways and athletic prowess made him popular with all ranks. But there was another, gentler side to him that expressed itself in a love of nature in general and of wild flowers in particular. He and Derrick, with their shared Scottish background, got on very well and remained firm friends afterwards. The Kashgar Vice-Consulship was George's first and only posting in the consular service.

Derrick and George were surprised to find that Kashgar was not really Chinese in character at all but an essentially Central Asian town. In its bazaars and dusty thoroughfares all sorts of exotic types rubbed shoulders with each other: Turkis, Kirghiz, Kalmuks, Kazaks, Tungans, Afghans and Mongols. Their dress was appropriately ethnic and the dominant religion was Islam. The Han Chinese were conspicuously in the minority here and had by no means fully consolidated their hold over the town and the surrounding region.

The British Consulate-General was situated on a bluff just

outside the town. It was a large, solid, fortress-like building, complete with battlements: a suitable monument to contemporary British power and prestige. Appropriately it bore the name of the building which previously occupied the same site: Chini Bagh, meaning Chinese Garden. Indeed, the ample terraced gardens were one of the delights of the place. Standing here, one could look across the green and chequered valley of a small river towards distant mountains. The Consulate was cool, clean and spacious within. There were soft chairs, rugs, books and a floor of wood instead of the mud that was usual in the region. The bathroom had a concrete tub and gadgets for heating water, and the bedrooms had spring beds. There was even a tennis court. Needless to say, this congenial haven of English comfort in such a distant land was keenly appreciated by the occasional weary and dusty traveller who found a moment's sanctuary there. 'All along the road I thought of the British Consulate ... for the memory of its cool, white-washed walls was a consolation out in the heat and dust of the plains,' wrote the American traveller and naturalist, Sudyam Cutting. The staff at Chini Bagh included a doctor, Chinese and Indian secretaries, Turki orderlies and an Escort of troops—often Hunza Scouts.

There was a Swedish Mission in Kashgar at the time of Derrick's arrival, but of far greater concern to him was the Soviet Consulate-General which was housed along with its considerable staff in an imposing building that had once been the abode of the late Tsar's representatives. Indeed, the Soviet border was little more than a stone's throw from Kashgar and the presence of such a large, powerful and expansionist nation, armed as it was with the ideological ambition of setting the East ablaze with the fire of proletarian revolution, naturally worried both the local Chinese authorities and the British, who had for a long time feared Russian designs on the Indian Jewel in the Imperial Crown. Kipling coined a term for the rival machinations of the Russians and the British in the East: the 'Great Game'—and at times the Great Game was played nowhere more intensely than at

Kashgar. Certainly, the Soviets kept a hawk-eye on all that was happening at Chini Bagh and were not at all reluctant to resort to dastardly underhand methods to outmanoeuvre their British rivals, attempting to infiltrate spies, to suborn members of the staff and even to intercept the official mail. And at the same time they did everything they could to undermine the British vis-à-vis the local Chinese adminis-trators. It would, on the other hand, be naïve to imagine that the British did not take counter-measures of their own. Certainly two of Derrick's immediate predecessors at Kashgar, Majors Percy Etherton and George Gillan, were highly enthusiastic players of the Great Game—and not untalented ones either. They had their own intelligence net-works and stratagems for foiling the plots of their Soviet opposite numbers.

His posting to Kashgar inevitably threw Derrick into the thick of the Great Game. Indeed, during his tour of duty there, relations between Britain and the Soviet Union reached a particularly low ebb and diplomatic relations were severed for two years. He complained in his reports of the large number of staff at the Soviet Consulate-General, citing fig-ures of thirty to forty 'Europeans', most of whom were nominally attached to the Trade Agency. His Soviet opposite number was a Mr. Posnikoff, whom he described as 'a man of gentlemanly habits and considerable education,' and as such much more 'tactful' than the sinister Max Doumpiss who had preceded him. He and George, however, saw little of Mr. Posnikoff and his staff, except at Chinese entertainments, though calls were exchanged to mark the resumption of relations between the two governments.

Derrick meanwhile found the province surrounding Kashgar under the control of a wiley yet able administrator named Yang Tseng-hsin. Governor Yang had held the reins of power for over fifteen years and though Derrick felt that his administration was 'startlingly corrupt in our eyes', he had at the same time to admit that it was 'by no means a bad one by local standards.' Yang's attitude to him personally was 'consistently friendly;' he did not like foreigners in general but he had come to appreciate that 'he has nothing to fear from the British and everything to fear from the Soviets'. It was Governor Yang who had put the impossible Doumpiss firmly in his place when he had impudently suggested that he, the Soviet Consul-General, should be regarded as senior to his British counterpart.

Local power in Kashgar itself was delegated to one of Governor Yang's favourites, a Tungan, or Chinese Moslem, named Ma Shao-wu, who was officially styled 'Taoyin'. Derrick at first found Taoyin Ma 'consistently friendly' too and he admired the firm attitude he took towards the Soviets. Taoyin Ma was not easy to deal with, however, as he tended to have definite views and to press them strongly. But, it was usually possible to agree finally upon some form of more or less reasonable compromise.

As Consul-General, Derrick's principal function was to look after the interests of British subjects in Chinese Turkestan. Mainly Indians who were involved in trade and financial activities there, they had for a long time enjoyed extraterritorial rights. Derrick's work meant making extensive tours from time to time, a form of duty that he was able to fulfil properly because George Sherriff could look after things at the Consulate-General in Kashgar while he was away.

In July 1928, on his return from Yarkand at the conclusion of a long tour that had taken him as far as Khotan and Keriya, Derrick received the disquieting news of Governor Yang's assassination. Yang had been distributing diplomas at a government college in Urumchi, the provincial capital, when he was gunned down by a gang of twenty dissidents led by Fan Yao-nan, his Foreign Affairs Commisioner. Fan had then hastened to the dead Governor's yamen or residency, intending to seize his seal of office, but had instead been captured there himself by Chin Shu-zen, the Taoyin of Urumchi, and brutally executed along with his henchmen. Chin was then duly elected the next Governor (or Chairman of the Province) by the Urumchi officials.

In Kashgar on 19 July Derrick called officially on Taoyin Ma to tender the British Government's sympathies, for Governor Yang had on the whole been a very good friend of British interests. He found Taoyin Ma clearly worried and wondered whether, with his patron gone, he might feel vulnerable to attack from his old rival, General Erh, who commanded the Chinese garrison in the New City some seven miles away from Kashgar itself. To show support, Derrick invited Taoyin Ma to feel free to ask for assistance if he felt that law and order were in danger of breaking down, though in reality he knew that there was little that he could effectively do to help. Ma seemed grateful for this gesture of moral support. In the event, there was no trouble in Kashgar. The local population went peaceably about their usual occupations and the only sign that there was anything unusual was that the city gates were closed a little early and slightly larger guards placed on them.

During the crisis, Derrick watched the Russians closely, for he received ominous reports that they were strengthening their forces on the border. 'It is extremely dangerous to prophesy, especially as to Bolshevik plans,' he wrote in one of his reports, 'but I think it unlikely that they will try to take control of this province, unless disorders break out. In the latter case, they might possibly send troops "to keep order" and then take them away.' Nothing untoward happened on this front either.

The new governor was initially less friendly towards Derrick than his predecessor had been. For a start, he contested the extraterritorial rights of British subjects in eastern Turkestan; then he closed the wireless station in Kashgar, which was the only rapid means of communication with British India that Derrick had; finally, in 1929, he told Derrick that he did not want him to come to Urumchi to pay an official call on him. Derrick knew that he could have insisted but at the same time he was well aware that it would be pointless to do so, for there were a thousand ways whereby a wiley Chinese autocrat could avoid anything that he desired to avoid. Behind all this, Derrick smelt the unmistakable odour of Soviet influence. Governor Chin continued to be 'tactless'—a word that frequently crops up in Derrick's official reports and apparently the strongest epithet in his political vocabulary—until the British agreed to supply him with quantities of munitions. He still stuck fast on the matter of British extraterritorial rights, however, though fortunately at this time there were few criminal cases in the province involving British subjects.

While at Kashgar Derrick also helped secure the release of the leader of a band of White Russian Cossacks who had languished in a Kulja prison cell for many years. Some £350 was transmitted from a Mrs. Gregory in England to Derrick and with this, 'in a purely unofficial way', he was able to pay compensation to 'certain aggrieved parties' and give the unfortunate Russian sufficient funds to travel to France.

Besides all the useful political work that he did, Derrick was also able to bring about a personal meeting while he was in Kashgar that was to have long-term and highly productive consequences.

In 1927, Frank Ludlow, a friend of Derrick, who had spent his working life in the Indian Education Service, retired in order to devote himself entirely to the love of his life: the study of birds and plants. He went first to Srinagar in Kashmir, intending to use this as his base for forays into the Himalayas in quest of specimens for the Natural History section of the British Museum. Knowing that he intended to make an expedition into the Tien Shan mountains, Derrick invited Lud, as he was known, to spend the winter of 1929–30 with him in Kashgar. Lud jumped at the chance and arrived at Chini Bagh in September. There Lud met George Sherriff for the first time.

Despite certain fundamental differences of temperament, both George and Lud shared a deep love of nature, of field sports and the open air. Going off together on hunting trips out of Kashgar, sometimes in Derrick's company, sometimes by themselves, the two men soon became good friends, a friendship that was to last for over twenty years and to form the basis for a number of highly successful specimen-collecting expeditions into remote parts of the Himalayas.

Lud has written the following of this time:

> Winters in Sinkiang are extremely cold with temperatures falling to many degrees below zero Fahrenheit, but the Consulate was a comfortable building well equipped with giant Russian stoves to withstand the subarctic temperatures, and time passed pleasantly enough. Often, during the long winter evenings, we talked about Tibet, a country to which Williamson was passionately devoted and to which, he said, he was determined to return as soon as his service in Sinkiang was over. I too had fallen in love with Tibet during the three years I had spent in Gyantse from 1923 to 1926, and Sheriff had also come under its spell on the Ladakh—Tibet frontier. So we extracted a promise from Williamson that when he had obtained the coveted post of Political Officer in Sikkim, Bhutan and Tibet, he would do all he could to obtain permission for us to travel in that country.

When Derrick left Kashagar on 4 October 1930, he took with him a great deal of experience that was to be of immense value in his subsequent career, notably insight into the convolutions of the Chinese official mind and the artful methods essential when dealing with it. He left just in time. An era of appalling bloodshed was about to break over Chinese Turkestan. George stayed behind for a while as Officiating Consul-General, but tendered his resignation when he found that official ears in Delhi and London were deaf to his warnings of Soviet designs upon the province.

IN 1931, AFTER A THIRD PERIOD OF LEAVE spent in Switzerland and England, Derrick became Acting Political Officer in Sikkim, thereby partially realizing the dreams he had entertained in wintry Turkestan. His work took him again to

Gyantse, where by happy coincidence my brother, Bill
Marshall, was the Captain of the 1/5th Mahratta Light
Infantry. Between June 1931 and October 1933, Bill was responsible for training twenty-five men of the Dalai Lama's
bodyguard (the so-called 'Royal Guards Regiment') in
machine-gunning and bombing. Yutok Se (later Depön) was
in command of the Tibetan contingent, while Jigme Taring, a
young Tibetan nobleman who had been educated at St. Paul's
School in Darjeeling, was deputed to act as interpreter and to
receive military training as well. Jigme and his wife Mary later
became lifelong friends of ours.

In 1932, Derrick went on leave for a fourth time. He visited
Jerusalem, Norway, Sweden and the Dalmatian Coast, before
going on to England, where he spent those happy days in
Torquay that I have already described.

After returning to India in the summer, Derrick was able
to fulfil another of his ambitions, a visit to Mount Kailas and
Lake Manasarovar in Western Tibet. The border between
Tibet and Tehri Garhwal had been in dispute for several
years, and the Government of India sent Derrick to tour the
disputed area, and to discuss the problems with Tibetan
officials in Gangtok. Derrick decided to invite Lud, and
together they spent an enjoyable two months touring the area
up to Mount Kailas, and studying the local bird and animal
life. As regards the political work, Derrick realised that such
matters could not be resolved by local officials, but the first
hand local knowledge he acquired was useful when he subsequently discussed the dispute in Lhasa.

Two months after returning from this tour, on 4th January
1933, Derrick was finally given the post he dearly wanted-
Political Officer in Sikkim. I was to join him in Gangtok just
a few months later.

3 Wedding in Gangtok

MY PASSAGE TO India passed pleasantly, for I got in with a bright crowd and there was much merrymaking, including sports and dancing. I remember too the bracing walks on the promenade deck, where there was no protection against the elements except for a little hessian strung from the railings. Things were particularly invigorating in the Bay of Biscay.

The ship was old and slow, perhaps on its final voyage, and we were ten days late arriving in Calcutta. Derrick, who had come down from Sikkim to meet me, had been obliged by urgent business to return to Gangtok, but before leaving he telephoned my brother Bill, then stationed with the 1/5th Mahrattas in the Lines at Alipore. Much to Bill's surprise (since he had no idea I was on my way out East), Derrick asked him to meet me off the boat. Although I took it in my stride, the vivid new sights, sounds and smells of India were overwhelming and I was grateful for Bill's familiar presence in the noise and confusion of the Calcutta crowds.

Bill booked me a four-berth compartment to myself on the evening train to Siliguri and saw me off.

'When the train's under way,' he chided me earnestly, 'get inside your compartment and lock the door—and on no account open it during the night, no matter how much banging and shouting there may be on the other side.'

At Siliguri I was met by a *chaprassy* (messenger) whom Derrick had sent down with a taxi. His name was Lugi and he looked splendid in his red uniform jacket trimmed with black velvet and his little hat of split bamboo sporting its peacock feather fixed with the official badge of the PO Sikkim. He also wore a kind of striped skirt of hand-woven material that came to just above the knees; his legs and feet were bare.

Lugi, who spoke no English (and I none of his language), handed me a letter from Derrick. 'Leave everything in the chaprassy's hands,' it read, 'and please also find enclosed an entry permit for Sikkim, which you'll be asked to show at the frontier.'

Excited as I was at the time by all the powerful impressions crowding in on me on my first encounter with India, I certainly registered the part about putting everything in the chaprassy's hands. What I didn't register was the message about the entry permit, which I stuffed away in a corner of my handbag and forgot about.

As I stood on the station platform I was accosted by three of the senior ladies attached to the Governor's entourage. They had looked me up and down from a distance for a good few moments, clearly eaten up with curiosity as to who might be of sufficient importance to have a Sikkim chaprassy sent a full seventy-five miles to meet them—an unheard-of privilege.

'I see you're going to stay with Mr. Williamson,' one of them ventured, half a question, half a statement. She then stood back, expecting me to be gushingly forthcoming, no doubt.

I'm afraid at that point a certain Scots obtuseness asserted itself. Aside from uttering a brief affirmative, I provided no further information, which clearly didn't satisfy my interrogators.

'How long are you staying for?' asked another.

'I really don't know,' I replied briskly—a true answer as it happened. 'Now please excuse me, I must get my breakfast.'

While I was having breakfast in the station restaurant, Lugi stowed my considerable luggage in the boot of the taxi and also bought some fish, as was customary, for the fish up at Gangtok were so full of bones as to be uneatable. After breakfast, we set off. For the first dozen or so miles the road ran across monotonously flat country, but I could see the hills looming up ahead and getting steadily closer. Of course we could only see the densely wooded foothills at that elevation, but I knew that behind them lurked great snow peaks and formidable glaciers.

Then, hardly before I knew it, we were actually into the hills and beginning to climb. All around us, towering ridges clothed with abundant vegetation, plunged precipitously down into the narrow valley-bed of the Teesta river that raced across tangled rocks on its southerly course. The road—it wasn't a road really so much as a rough track along which the valiant taxi could crawl at a snail's pace, with much honking of its horn whenever we came to a bend—wound its way along the sides of the valley, often with a drop of hundreds of feet down to the river on one side, and also crossed the river by way of a suspension bridge. It was clear that this was a notorious place for landslips and other hazards, but thankfully everything went well, including the occasional encounter with a mule train coming down from Tibet with yak wool.

Coming eventually to the frontier post at Rungpo, the officials there naturally enough wanted to see my entry permit, which I'd absent-mindedly put away. Unfortunately, the language difficulties meant that I didn't get their message. They, however, could see that I must be a bona fide visitor as I was accompanied by a Sikkim chaprassy, so they let me through after I'd signed my name on a piece of paper.

On this last leg of the journey I was really nervous. Of course I was wondering whether things would be the same between Derrick and myself. Would he have changed? More worrying in a way, would he find that I had changed? Gradually, with what for me was agonizing slowness, the poor little hard-labouring taxi ground in low gear up towards the Sangkakhola dak bungalow, where I knew Derrick would be waiting for me. As we approached, the door of the bungalow opened and Derrick appeared and all my worries dissolved.

How delighted we were to see each other again. We drove

on up to Gangtok in his Morris, talking happily the whole way. Derrick's sister, Bess was with us. She was married to Robert Toplis, the High Commissioner for Bihar and Orissa, who was shortly to retire. She had come up to the hills with her two children and their nanny to get away from the oppressive heat of the plains.

At first sight, the Residency struck me as looking just like an English country house, except that it had a corrugated iron roof of a dull reddish colour. The verandahs, where meals were taken when the weather was suitable, were hung with wistaria. The grounds were extensive and descended in three tiers to two lily-ponds. On the top terrace there were spacious lawns, a fish-pond and the great flag-pole where the Union Jack fluttered proudly when the Political Officer was in residence. The flag went with him on tour, when it was hoisted at each camp. A hill rose up at the back, concealing the servants' quarters. All around there were masses of flowers, trees and tree-ferns. But the crowning glory of the place was the magnificent view that it commanded of the Kanchenjunga range to the west. Claude White, the first PO Sikkim, who had built the Residency between 1888 and 1890, had certainly chosen a perfect setting for it.

Later that first afternoon, Derrick and I strolled in the grounds of the Residency.

'Well, Peggy, how do you find it here?'

'It's strange,' I replied, 'but I feel perfectly at home.'

At that moment a policeman appeared and came over to Derrick; I began to move away, thinking it must be official business, but Derrick drew me back.

'You may be able to help the officer, Peggy. It seems as though a terrible crime has been perpetrated,' he said with an ironic smile.

'Oh?'

'Yes. Down at the frontier. Apparently a lady of British appearance crossed over into Sikkim today without an entry permit.'

'Was that me?'

'It must have been. But I sent a permit down to Siliguri for you. Surely Lugi remembered to hand it over?'

'Oh, that!' I exclaimed, suddenly seeing what must have happened. 'I pushed it into my handbag and forgot all about it.'

Fortunately the policeman was very kind. I was able to produce the crucial document and he accepted my explanation and left.

DURING MY FIRST DAYS AT THE RESIDENCY, Derrick and I didn't discuss marriage at all. He had, however, consulted Dr. Hendricks about the matter of my acclimatization to the altitude. Dr. Hendricks, who was Anglo-Indian and a very fine GP, came to see me and suggested I rest for the next three weeks, only going for a morning ride with Derrick. It was difficult especially as I was very eager to get to know the place, but I thought it best to follow the doctor's advice.

When the three weeks were up, Derrick asked me: 'Do you think you'd like to try a short tour now?'

'I certainly would!' I replied enthusiastically.

Mr. and Mrs. Waters were visiting us at that time. They were from Virginia in the United States, and had previously stayed with Derrick in Kashgar. The four of us therefore set off and trekked up to the Penlong pass, which at 7,000 feet above sea level is 1,000 feet higher than Gangtok. Then we descended to 2,000 feet at Dikchu before climbing again up to 5,000 feet, where we stayed at the Singhik dak bungalow, which faced the Kanchenjunga range with its many shining snow-capped peaks. We spent a very pleasant three days there. Dr. Hendricks had given me medicine to take if the altitude affected me, but I did not need it. I felt extremely well the whole time. The wonderful Sikkimese scenery with its exotic butterflies and flowers, the wayside grog shops, and all the fascinating people that we met made me completely forget about myself.

At this time, the reigning Maharaja of Sikkim was Sir Tashi Namgyal, who was married to a lady of the Tibetan Ragashar family. They had six children. The girls were called Coocoola, Kula, and Jean-la, and the boys, Pejo, Thondup and George-la. Tragically, the eldest son, Pejo, was later killed while night-flying in India during the Second World War. His brother, Thondup, who was living in a Buddhist monastery when I first came to Gangtok was many years later to become the next ruler, adopting the title of *Chögyal*, which means 'Protector of the Dharma'. Most of the Sikkimese people are Buddhists following the Mahayana tradition of Tibet.

Derrick greatly admired the Buddhists. 'They really live their religion,' he used to say, and he thought it as good as our own. He in fact refused to allow a Christian church to be built in Gangtok during his time there.

Although resident in Sikkim, Derrick's responsibilities also extended to Bhutan and Tibet. He had an Assistant for Bhutan, Raja Sonam Tobgye Dorji, who was also Prime Minister of Bhutan. His wife, Rani Chuni Dorji, was the sister of the Maharaja of Sikkim and spoke excellent English, an unusual accomplishment at that time for any lady from the Himalayas. In her youth she had of her own initiative packed her bags and gone off to Dehra Dun to get herself a good British education. Tobgye and Chuni, who had a house in nearby Kalimpong, were great friends of Derrick's and later of mine.

One day shortly after our return from the small tour over towards Kanchenjunga, Derrick found me in the cottage in the Residency grounds. He seemed a little shy or preoccupied, talking generalities for a time before turning directly towards me and coming to the point.

'Well,' he said, 'will you marry me now, Peggy?'

I was in no doubt at all as to the answer to that question. That uncanny feeling of being at home that I had experienced on first arriving in Sikkim had strengthened during the days that followed, as had my feelings for Derrick.

'Yes,' I replied, smiling. 'Now that I know I can stand the height.'

'Good. But we must get cracking with the arrangements if
you are to come on tour with me. It's May already and I want
to make a start in June, before the monsoon sets in.'

THE AMBITIOUS TOUR projected for the coming summer had
been much in the air throughout my time in Gangtok. When
he had taken over as Political Officer in Sikkim, Derrick had
written to both His Highness the Maharaja of Bhutan and to
His Holiness the Dalai Lama of Tibet, presenting his compli-
ments and introducing himself. He received formal replies
from both, their respective letters bearing the same date: the
seventh day of the twelfth month of the Water-monkey year,
that is, 1 February, 1933.

Thanking Derrick for his letter of 19 January, His Holiness
wrote:

> I am very glad to note the assurance that during the
> tenure of your office, it will be your endeavour to
> further cement the friendly relations existing between
> Britain and Tibet. You also express that you will
> have the pleasure of meeting me in the near future
> and that you will make your acquaintance with me.
> It would be very good if you could come to Lhasa
> as soon as possible.

The Maharaja also wrote to Derrick in similar vein:

> I am very glad that you are keeping good health and
> that your affairs are in prosperous condition like the
> moon in ascendance ... Now you have again come
> as Political Officer in Sikkim and I cherish the
> greatest hope of being able to meet with you. It is
> therefore my earnest request that this year you will
> kindly arrange to come to my capital to meet me.

Armed with these invitations, Derrick wrote to the Foreign
Secretary of the Government of India, strongly urging that,
in view of the highly personal nature of the work of the
Political Officer in Sikkim, he be allowed to respond positively

to both invitations and visit Bhutan and Tibet that year. 'Personal contact and friendships made now will be of immense value throughout the whole of my time as the Political Officer in Sikkim,' he wrote. As for the financial side, he would not ask the Government of India for an additional grant to cover his tour of Bhutan, 'although it will entail the exercise of the most rigid economy, the expenses of the visit will be met from my sanctioned budget grants.' Tibet, however, was another proposition. If his visit there was to be a success, he would have to give lavish presents in Lhasa, the capital, and generally be able to cut a bit of a figure. He therefore asked for an additional grant of 10,000 rupees to cover that part of the projected tour. Finally, as 'no presents are as much appreciated as firearms,' he asked to be provided with thirty rifles and six thousand rounds of ammunition. Persuaded by Derrick's arguments, the Government of India gave its permission.

And so, with this exciting first official tour in prospect, Derrick and I became officially engaged. As was customary, a notice was put in *The Statesman*. After it had appeared, Jenny Visser-Hoof, the wife of the Netherlands Ambassador to India, told me: 'You don't know how many *chota hazri* sets [morning tea services] were broken in Delhi the morning the announcement appeared! You see, everyone thought that Derrick was a confirmed bachelor.'

Derrick's old bachelor friends, Ludlow and Sherriff, were also greatly surprised when they heard the news. Lud was unable to come to the wedding, but George agreed to be Derrick's best man.

I needed a wedding dress and so Bess Toplis and I went over to Darjeeling and found a tailor. It was quite a simple dress of soft satin, with no lace trimmings. The only lace I wore for my wedding was the lovely veil I was sent by the nuns at Ranchi.

I didn't feel at all nervous or apprehensive when our wedding day, 22 May, dawned. One surprising thing did happen before the ceremony, however. I was getting ready in my room, which had previously served as Derrick's dressing-room, when he appeared in the doorway.

'Look, my braces have broken,' he said. 'Can you do something about it?'

'Yes, of course,' I said, but afterwards realized that you are not supposed to see your future husband before the ceremony.

The wedding ceremony was held in the White Memorial Hall, which Claude White had had built as a place where people could meet. For the occasion, the Maharaja and the Maharani, with characteristic kindness, had arranged for it to be beautifully decorated. They had lent their own splendid blue carpet and gold chairs with pink brocade upholstery, and laid on a quite dazzling array of flowers. The whole place had been completely transformed.

The weather was less kind, however. It rained in the morning and Derrick arrived at the White Hall riding on a pony with George Sherriff walking alongside holding an umbrella over him.

The ceremony was conducted by Dr. Graham of the Scottish Presbyterian Mission in Kalimpong, who was famous in the district for his many good works. He had founded orphanages, schools, hospitals and arts-and-crafts centres. By 1933, he was quite old and a widower. He had been a Moderator of the Church of Scotland, and as Derrick and I were both of Scottish blood we felt he was the perfect person to marry us. That day he was magnificently dressed in silk stockings and buckled shoes, with lace ruffles at the collar and wrists.

None of my family attended the wedding as my brother Bill had recently been posted to the North-West Frontier and was unable to come. I was therefore given away by Robert Toplis, Derrick's brother-in-law. My chief bridesmaid was Tashi-la, the elder daughter of Raja and Rani Dorji, supported by the Maharaja's daughters. Dr. Hendrick's children acted as attendants.

The rain had stopped when we emerged from the White

Hall after the ceremony, and Derrick and I returned by car to the Residency in sunshine, followed by the rest of the party. We then had a modest luncheon party provided by Robert Toplis and prepared by Pinjo, our cook. Champagne had been sent up from Calcutta for the occasion. Apart from our European friends, the Maharaja and Maharani were present, together with Raja and Rani Dorji, and the headmen of the various divisions of Sikkim; in all, about thirty people.

All the people who had not attended this first luncheon were invited to a garden party that was held on the Residency lawn later in the afternoon. About three hundred people from all over Sikkim came to that. Finally, there was a dinner party in the evening. We had twenty-three guests at the Residency that night. I have no idea where they all slept but next morning they left. Derrick and I were alone at last.

THE NECESSARY STORES and other requisites for our great tour of Bhutan and Tibet had long ago been ordered from Calcutta and safely received. The system was in fact that the stores were ordered once a year, as this was the most economical way of doing things. It was expensive if anything had to be sent up specially, even something as trivial as a reel of cotton. Derrick had also been down to Calcutta to buy the numerous gifts that it was customary to present while on tour. These ranged from a complete three-piece suite of furniture down to simple things like torchlights. The 10,000 rupee grant from the Government in New Delhi provided for the purpose was woefully inadequate, and we had to supplement it from our own resources. After a tour such as this, any presents received were deemed to be government property, although if we wished to retain anything for ourselves or for the Residency we were allowed to buy it back from the Government.

As for clothing, although I knew that we should be travelling to great altitudes and crossing snowbound passes, I didn't take anything other than clothes I had brought out from England. Certainly no special down jackets or stout

Alpine climbing boots. I took woollies, tweed skirts and jackets, cotton jackets and frocks, jumper suits, jodhpurs, breeches and puttees; also a few pairs of shoes, nailed boots and, for special occasions when I might have to meet a high lama and need to be very decorous, a long pleated skirt of French tweed.

On the morning following our wedding, Samdup, Derrick's personal manservant and friend who had served him for ten years, presented himself and offered me the keys of the *godown* (stores).

'But I don't want them, Samdup,' I told him. 'You've always given out everything until now. I'd be pleased if you would continue to do so. But I'd like you to have a key cut for me so that, if I want to go into the godown, I don't have to send for you.' I also added, 'I don't know what arrangements have been made for ordering stores for this tour, but I have a feeling that when we go on another tour we'll arrange things a little differently.'

I must say the Samdup was marvellous and helped me enormously to get into the swing of things. He had the uncanny knack of being able to anticipate whatever I wanted.

Our cook, Pinjo, who was also coming on tour with us, was a private servant too, though he had been employed by a number of previous Political Officers. He'd rather blotted his copy book during Colonel 'Eric' Bailey's time, however. One evening, Mrs. Bailey was holding a dinner party at the Residency. All the guests were assembled and waiting, but time went by and no one came to announce that dinner was served. Then word reached Mrs. Bailey's ear that Pinjo was lying dead drunk on the kitchen floor! Mrs. Bailey, however, had great presence of mind. She opened up the godown and told all her guests to go in and choose a tin of something for dinner. Thus disaster was skilfully averted.

Pinjo knew that this had been reported to me, for one day he turned to me and said: 'Memsahib, Pinjo will never get drunk while you and the Sahib are here.' However, I went without forewarning to the servants' quarters on one occasion and there caught Pinjo redhanded, drinking *marwa*, the local brew. He must have noticed the look of surprise on my face, for he at once said: 'It's all right, Memsahib. Pinjo only drinks two of these a day and he will never let you down.' And he was as good as his word.

He was an excellent cook, again thanks to Mrs. Bailey. She had had the good sense to have him sent down to Firpo's in Calcutta to be properly trained. My relationship with him worked very well because it was founded on trust.

On 29 May 1933, just a week after our wedding, I got up, dressed and busied myself with my final preparations for our journey. I really did not know what to expect. Would I be up to the rigours of the journey? What hazards and adventures might await us in high and remote places? To such questions I could provide no answers, but I did know that I was entirely content and would not have wished to be anywhere else in all the world.

4 Honeymoon in Bhutan

DERRICK AND I did not set off from the Residency until after we had had an early lunch. This was to allow a party with about twenty mules carrying our personal baggage, the servants' kit and some of the stores to travel ahead and prepare a camp for us at Karponang. Besides this, another party including about seventy coolies had also gone on ahead about two days previously carrying the bulk of the stores and office equipment, camping gear, presents for Bhutanese and Tibetan dignitaries, plus our cinematograph and gramophone. All this was to be taken to Yatung, just over the Tibetan border in the Chumbi Valley, where it could be later sorted out. Some would then be forwarded to Gyantse and Lhasa to await our arrival; the remainder would travel with us. Our own travelling party included our medical officer, Captain David Tennant of the Indian Medical Service, then Acting Surgeon at Gyantse, and Rai Bahadur Norbhu Dhondup, Derrick's personal assistant. There were the clerks and our servants, with their wives and children—and of course we could not leave Derrick's beloved Springer Spaniel, Bruce.

As our ponies began to climb out of Gangtok, my spirits soared. I felt a wonderful sense of freedom and adventure in leaving British India behind and travelling into new and undiscovered countries. At first our road was a good one, wide enough to accommodate a Baby Austin; later, however, it dwindled to a mere track, rocky, narrow and steadily ascending through dense bamboo jungle and giant rhododendron trees.

Although the weather held for most of the day's march, about two miles out from Karponang a blanket of dense cloud descended and we were lucky to get into camp just before the rain came down in torrents. That night we slept on camp-beds, a great change from the spring beds we had at the Residency. Derrick had thoroughly spoiled me, however: he had a little mattress made for my camp-bed so that I would be more comfortable. Another luxury we brought along was a six-foot canvas bath, supplied by the Army & Navy Stores in Calcutta.

The next day, having left the bamboo country behind us, we were regaled with a feast of colour as we climbed through a rhododendron forest in glorious flower. There were creams and reds, and later more reds, terracotta, salmon and pink flowers.

About three miles out of Karponang, we looked back over two ridges and through the field-glasses made out the Palace, the Secretariat and the *Lhakang* (temple) back down in Gangtok. Then we continued our climb, passing many steep precipices on the way and a gloomy region of 'blasted pine forest' where all the trees were wizened and hung with beards of moss and lichen. Fortunately the weather held all morning. Looking up we could see the sun shining on the river that came cascading down through pine-covered ridges where snow lay in all the crevices. We also came upon some pretty black birds with red tails and heads streaked with white. Higher still there were yak grazing; the herdsmen's tents were pitched near by. These were made of yak hair and looked very greasy. Then at the top we came to the Changu Lake.

The dwarf rhododendrons growing on the steep slopes in the vicinity were not in flower as it was too cold. We burned rhododendron wood in camp at the end of that day's march. It takes some time to get going but when it does it burns with a fierce heat. The fire quickly dried out our damp clothing and lifted our spirits, for although the weather had held during the morning, in the afternoon it had rained heavily.

The next morning we followed the stony pathway up to the Natu-la or Natu pass—altitude, 14,300 feet—our gateway into Tibet. Looking back I could see the twisting path we had just climbed, while all around us were magnificent snowy mountains. There were lakes too, covered with ice and, far below, in the hidden depths of some deep valley, I could hear the distant roar of a turbulent river. At that moment I truly felt I was on the top of the world!

We encountered deep snow on the Natu-la, which we reached around 10.30 am, and our ponies floundered in it. Mine sank so deep that I rolled off and had to trudge the last hundred yeards on foot. At the top of the pass, where I arrived breathless but exhilarated, we were rewarded for our efforts with a splendid view. The imposing mountains of Tibet ranged away to our left, culminating in the splendid snow peak of Chomolhari; and Bhutan lay to our right, with a deep valley below.

As we descended from the pass, coolies cleared the snow and slush from our path. We were now truly in Tibetan territory, so it seemed appropriate to pause at the bottom for tea.

I had perhaps better say something about Tibetan tea, as it is so important to the Tibetans. Although better quality Indian tea could have been imported with ease and sold far more cheaply, the Tibetans had developed an insatiable taste for Chinese black tea. It was imported in brick form, often sewn inside skins for safety during transit. A lump of tea was broken off and boiled from cold in water. A knob of butter was then added, also some salt and soda. The soda prevented the butter floating on the surface. The brew—really a kind of broth—was then churned in a long wooden cylinder and reheated. Kettles of this were always on hand in Tibetan households, just as samovars were in Russia. The Tibetans drank innumerable cups of it throughout the day, for they found it very sustaining, especially in the cold climate. Well made, I too found it a delicious drink.

Later we rode on along a narrow track that wound through

sweet-smelling pine woods. Unfamiliar wild flowers could be seen on every side, while sunlight sparkled on the water of the torrents that came tumbling down the mountainside behind us to join the river running in the valley below. That day we stayed at the dak bungalow at Champithang, one of a number of pleasant little buildings put up for the benefit of official travellers by the Government of India. It commanded a fine view of snow-capped mountains. That night we burnt pine wood on our fire, which crackled heartily. We were up and away at eight o'clock the next morning, travelling mainly downhill through more pine forest. Looking briefly behind, I could see both the Jelep and Natu passes.

As we approached Yatung, we were met by a small reception committee composed of Rai Sahib Bo, the Agency doctor, Mr. Pemba, the Chief Clerk, and several others. The Tibetan Trade Agent was indisposed, we were informed, but sent his greetings and would we like to visit him in his own house? Long Tibetan trumpets boomed, accompanied by *gyelings*, a kind of bell-mouthed clarinet or oboe.

Having made our way beside the Chumbi river to the TTA's house, the gentleman himself met us at the door and cordially invited us to enter a rather dismal inner room. There we were offered Indian tea. I preferred the Tibetan tea that was later served to us in little jade cups, though it had a film of butter that had to be blown away before one could drink it. Afterwards we were served a Tibetan lunch, which had to be eaten with chopsticks. As we left, the trumpets and gyelings again sounded. Finally, we cantered on beside the river to the bungalow of the British Trade Agent, passing through a triumphal arch proclaiming WELCOME. All the people rushed out to see us and a detachment of Mahrattas was drawn up, which Derrick inspected.

The bungalow itself was altogether delightful and had a garden where lupins and other flowers were growing, reminding me of an English garden. We spent twelve happy days there, which Derrick had planned as our honeymoon, for back in Gangtok we had had virtually no time to ourselves.

Paro guest house.

Yatung – the British Trade Agency.

(Opposite) Paro Dzong, with bridge in foreground.

Paro Bridge

Paro Penlop with Tennant, Samdup behind.

Masked dancers at Paro.

*Taktsang Monastery,
perched above the Paro
Valley.*

*Drugye Dzong, Paro
Valley.*

*Ashi Wangmo, Maharani
and Ashi Peden.*

*Maharaja of Bhutan,
Tennant and self.*

(Opposite) Archers at Paro.

At Bumthang: Derrick, Dasho Gyurme Dorji, Sherriff, self, Raja Dorji, Norbhu and Ludlow.

In camp, with Sherriff, Ludlow, self and Tennant.

Rani Dorji, self and Raja Dorji.

Self in Dandy.

Yaks on Monla-karchung Pass.

I had to learn one lesson during our honeymoon that few brides have to learn: how to use a rifle. Derrick was adamant that I do this in case we had to visit the notoriously lawless province of Kham. Rifles were the only arms we carried and what a kick they had! I never anticipated the violence of it.

The outstanding day of our stay at Yatung was 3 June, when the King's birthday was celebrated in fine style. Derrick attired himself in full levee dress and went down to the local football-ground to take the salute. Afterwards he presented a decoration to the local postmaster that he had been awarded in the New Year's Honours List. We were thirteen to lunch that day, all Tibetans save for two Nepalese, Derrick and myself.

Later there were sports on the hockey-field, when various races were run. The military held a 'chariot' race and the ladies were persuaded to overcome their shyness and enter a 'straight' race. I personally enjoyed the childrens' races most of all. There was something about those young Tibetans that reminded me strongly of English children—those cheeky grins, perhaps! For the first time in my life I was asked to distribute the prizes, something I enjoyed as I had already begun to like the Tibetans a great deal.

Having said goodbye all round, we left Yatung and, dropping slightly all the time, travelled on beside the Chumbi river in glorious morning sunshine. Wheat and barley grew in abundance all about and the colour of the landscape was beautiful. After stopping for lunch, we crossed into Bhutan by way of a small bridge, the Lang Marpa, and from there twisted up and away from the Chumbi river into another valley, where we encountered both deciduous and coniferous trees that yielded here and there to the occasional patch of open grass. There were a lot of wild flowers, notably irises.

For the next six weeks we were to cross nearly the whole of Bhutan from west to east, and a pass was crossed on average about every third march. The scenery was magnificent: great rolling hills clothed with dense forest and intersected by deep valleys.

At Sharithang (11,350 feet), our first halting place in

Bhutan, we found a huge WELCOME sign and a beautiful camp prepared for us. An avenue of firs led up to a group of excellent huts built of split bamboo and other woods, with green fir branches covering the walls. The roofs were of laths, weighted down with heavy stones. There were also juniper hedges to provide privacy and protection against the wind, and blazing fires to warm us. All our camps in Bhutan were as good, even if we were only to stop for a single night.

We continued our journey, crossing two more high passes at about 14,000 feet. Again, there were many wild flowers; primulas, cowslips, marsh marigolds, periwinkles and dwarf rhododendrons of white, purple and red. Eventually we dropped into Damthang, at the head of the Ha valley. Here we were met by our friend Tobgye (Raja Dorji) who, in addition to his various other functions, was also the local *dzongpön* or district governor. He was to accompany and look after us throughout our stay in Bhutan, and he was ever a model of efficiency and thoughtfulness. Nothing was too small to be beneath his notice and nothing was too much trouble for him to undertake.

Later I asked Tobgye about the great effort that was being made to ensure our comfort.

'Maharaja's orders,' he replied tersely, as though there were nothing more to say.

'Yes, I know it must be the Maharaja's orders,' I persisted, 'but admit it: it was Chuni and yourself who thought of it, surely?'

After considerable prompting, he did finally concede that it had been their idea. 'We wanted this trip to be your honeymoon,' he said.

What thoughtfulness—and what a marvellous honeymoon!

THE SUN SHONE BRILLIANTLY as we rode through Damthang village the next morning. The few houses were large and rambling, built of mud and stone, with lathed roofs and prettily carved wooden window-frames. We rode for some seven miles down that richly cultivated valley, and at each hamlet the locals burnt juniper as a form of auspicious greeting. As we approached Ha we were met by a cheerful company of schoolboys of assorted ages, all wearing purple or green *chubas* (tunics), who walked ahead of us into the village, where again a band composed of monks played us in. The monks were perched with their instruments upon the roof of the local *dzong*, an imposing, square-built edifice standing in a courtyard surrounded by outer defensive structures. These fortresses dominate the main valleys of Bhutan in much the same way as castles did in Europe during the Middle Ages.

We were accommodated in the local guest-house, which enjoyed a peaceful and picturesque situation beside the river. It had been rebuilt and generally enlarged since Derrick had last visited Ha with Colonel Bailey in 1925. It had a double roof, and the outer walls were gaily painted in red, white and blue, while the inner walls had been adorned with painted flowers and various 'lucky signs'. Although these colours were vivid, they nevertheless blended harmoniously. The windows were glassless, but had sliding wooden panels, painted to match the walls, which could be drawn across at night.

At the guest-house we were greeted by Frank Ludlow and George Sherriff, who had come to Bhutan ahead of us in search of botanical specimens. I was pleased to be able to tell George that I had found a specimen of a large white poppy (*Meconopsis imperialis*) that he had asked me to get for him, and that I'd also seen the blue poppy.

At Derrick's request, George and Lud had been granted special permission by the Maharaja to collect botanical specimens in Bhutan, but in order to avoid unnecessary comment by officials not accustomed to European visitors, His Highness had considered it better that they should travel from Ha to Bumthang as members of our party. Altogether they were with us for over a month. They were discreet and sensitive travelling companions—they even used to remove their boots so as not to disturb Derrick and me when they were moving about in the early morning. They went off at the crack of dawn and we rarely saw them again until dinner time. When we eventually left Bhutan for Tibet, they spent a further month in eastern Bhutan before crossing into Tibet by way of the Boden-la to Lhakhang Dzong, having obtained permission from the Tibetan Government to go plant-hunting as far as Gyantse. This was to be the first of a series of remarkable natural history expeditions that the two friends made in the eastern Himalayas and southern Tibet, and of it Ludlow has written:

> Our collection of five hundred gatherings of plants was small compared with those made on subsequent expeditions. Perhaps the most interesting find was the discovery of *Meconopsis superba*, previously known in the wild only from the type-collection of 1884. At the end of this journey, Sherriff and I decided on a plan of campaign for the future. In brief, this was to work gradually eastwards through Tibet along the main Himalayan range, each succeeding journey overlapping its predecessor, until we reached the great bend of the Tsangpo. Thus ... we hoped to obtain valuable information concerning the distribution of plants. In addition ... the collection of seeds and living plants was also very much in our minds, and also the collection of birds, as the avifauna of the country we proposed to visit was totally unknown.

WE PAUSED FOR FIVE DAYS at Ha, much of that time spent very enjoyably trying to master the Bhutanese longbow. We had no hope of matching the skill of the locals, however. About seventy of the best of them gave a great archery display in our honour, and they were most adept at hitting the targets, even at a range of a hundred and fifty yards. They took enormous pleasure in their sport, for they danced about and sang a great deal, brandishing their weapons and exhorting their shafts to fly straight to the mark. What a handsome people they were, so full of energy and good humour!

Every archer was clad in his best chuba (called *kho* in Bhutan), which looks shorter than the Tibetan equivalent and is worn hitched up at the waist so as to leave the legs free and better able to negotiate the precipitous terrain of their native land. The fold at the waist forms a roomy pocket in which all the necessities of life, including food, may be carried.

A Bhutanese wife will spend a great deal of time weaving the colourful and intricately patterned material from which her husband's chuba is made, and even an everyday garment may represent the labour of months. Thus the chuba is at once a practical piece of clothing and a work of art. The women's chubas or *kiras* were worn full-length to the ankle and held at the shoulders by a pair of silver or gilt brooches linked by a chain. Both men and women wore their hair cropped short.

One morning it poured with rain, so instead of practising archery we went to the dzong and visited the temple inside it. We also saw the storerooms. When the rain cleared, the bowmen who were with us sang and danced on the steps of the dzong for the benefit of our cameras. Then they led the way with great pomp and ceremony to the sports-field, where a huge crowd had gathered to watch a contest of archery between the north valley and the south valley. In the afternoon we watched boxing and wrestling by the boys of Tobgye's excellent school. This was run by a young man who had been trained in India, and instruction was given both in English and in Hindi. Finally, after dinner, a huge fire was lit upon the guest-house lawn and a display of Bhutanese dancing was given. First the men danced, then the women, and finally both together, singing merry and melancholy songs as they did so.

On our final day in Ha, we watched an unusual way of fishing. One line of boys, beating the water with sticks, drove the fish downstream to where another line of boys were waiting in a 'V' formation. The latter then funnelled the fish into the wide mouth of a tapering bamboo basket.

Derrick, of course, was a great *shikari* (sportsman). He'd be off on his tummy whenever he got an opportunity, stalking some form of game. He was therefore very pleased to be able to get a day's sport in at Ha with Tobgye, Lud, Tennant, and Norbhu. They beat an almost perpendicular hillside and managed to bag a *serow* (goat antelope) and three musk deer. I also went down the valley with my rifle but only manged to get a small bird.

A HUGE CAVALCADE of men and transport set off the next morning for the two-day journey to Paro, our next destination. We first rode up through pine and deciduous forest to the Chi Lai pass (12,420 feet), then dismounted and negotiated the steep down-gradient to Chang-na-na. We got in just as an almighty storm broke over us. Hail, thunder and lightning proclaimed the onset of the monsoon. Some men were waiting for us there with brightly caparisoned mules, having been sent out by the district governor of Paro, the *Penlop*.

Setting out early the next day, we wound round various spur heads on our way to Paro. Tobgye led on his mule, complete with bodyguard. The rest of us followed in single file, each mule led by a Bhutanese attendant and a second servant following behind. Our servants brought up the rear. The view from the top was stunning. Range after range of green velvety hills stretched away to the horizon, while Paro itself lay in the valley below with its enormous dzong and guest-house.

About three miles from Paro we were greeted by a guard of honour dressed in bright silk chubas and armed with exotic weaponry: swords in silver scabbards, rhinoceros-hide shields and burnished steel helmets. There were also dancers and musicians playing Tibetan trumpets and, after a reception where we were given ceremonial tea and rice, they preceded us down the hill past the Gorina monastery into Paro itself, leading the way with singing and dancing.

It was now clear to me that there were no settlements in Bhutan that could qualify for the name of town; nor were there any shops or bazaars. By local standards, therefore, Paro was a metropolis, over twenty miles in length. Little of this area was built up, however, for each house was surrounded by a sizeable tract of land upon which the family could grow enough food to support itself and a little over to barter for other goods.

The fact that Bhutan had sufficient land for all and consequently suffered from no population problem meant, moreover, that the people could enjoy an unusually happy way of life. As they could grow or barter all that they needed for subsistence, they had little or no use for money, and thus were largely free from its attendant evils. Avarice, crime, poverty and begging were conspicuously absent. What peace and joy after all the manifold problems of the plains! A true Shangri-la.

But for Derrick and me, entering Bhutan had not only been like stepping into a charged world; it had also been like stepping into the past. The costumes and way of life seemed to us like life in the Middle Ages. There was a similar love of colour, of pageantry and of the martial arts; a distinctly feudal system of social organization prevailed; and, of course, religion played a large part in the lives of all the people, from the humblest to the most exalted. Large bastions were also sited at every important centre, and the green and pleasant landscape was sprinkled with friendly homesteads, many of them fairly prosperous in appearance.

The Paro Penlop (Governor) turned out to be a fat, bald and amiable man in his mid-thirties and unmarried. Derrick had first met him in 1925 and he seemed to be genuinely delighted to see us. He was also a man of many talents, for he had himself designed the guest-house in which we were lodged. This was a beautiful, tall, pagoda-like building, brightly painted and sporting gargoyles on the roof. We were told that it was modelled on the heavenly abode of Guru Rinpoché (Padmasambhava). Our quarters were on the first floor, the ground floor being given over to storage and the top floor to shrine-rooms. The rest of our party occupied the cottages built into the four corners of the inner surrounding wall.

The Penlop was the grandson of the late Maharaja of Bhutan and by rank the second person in the land. He enjoyed almost absolute power within his own domain but was generally regarded as a benevolent administrator by the standards prevalent in Bhutan at the time. He did not share Derrick's love of hunting, his chief passion being to organize dances by his soldiers, of which we witnessed several displays. It was extremely polished dancing and much more entertaining than the lama dancing I had watched in Gangtok. The dancers wore attractive and unusual costumes. Those at one of the displays we attended had crossover pieces of silk about six inches wide, with faces painted on them, and small capes. Their colourful silk skirts looked rather like ballet skirts but underneath they wore a cloth painted to look like a tigerskin and below that a pair of shorts. Finally they donned grotesque animal masks and carried large hand-drums. They performed all kinds of steps, including quite complicated pirouettes, to the accompaniment of the music of a small band.

At Paro too there was a great deal of archery, and we put on cinema shows, though these had to be brief as Derrick's projector was worked by batteries which could not be recharged until we reached Lhasa. In the popularity ratings, Charlie Chaplin invariably had the edge on Fritz the Cat. This was the same wherever we showed the films, in both Sikkim and Bhutan, and later in Tibet.

The dzong at Paro is an enormous building perched on the summit of a cliff that overlooks the Paro river. It contains a monastery with a large, pillared assembly hall and numerous courtyards. As it is also protected by stout outworks, it would be virtually impregnable against all but modern weaponry.

One day, we made an excursion to the famous 'Tiger's Nest' monastery of Tak Tsang. It is situated about eight miles from Paro, perched like a stork's nest—or rather a series of storks' nests—on a cleft in a sheer precipice hundreds of feet high. It is really a collection of wide-gabled buildings connected by steep stairways and ladders. I could certainly appreciate its advantages for spiritually inclined people who might wish to get well away from the hurly-burly of everyday life in order to devote themselves to contemplation.

We had planned to stay four days in Paro but this had to be extended by one day as the result of a rather tragic turn of events. One night the Penlop came again to dinner and afterwards we were all settling ourselves to watch another cinema show when a breathless messenger rushed into the room. He informed the Penlop that the Tulku of Gangten, the incarnate lama who also served as the *dzongpön* of Thimpu, had been taken ill. The Penlop would not stay but left at once, we cancelled the cinema show and also the small fireworks display that had been planned to follow it. We also decided that it would now be impolitic to leave the following day as planned.

We finally left Paro on 20 June. The Paro Penlop accompanied us for the first leg of our onward journey, bringing his bodyguard along as well. Then after giving us tea and saffron-rice on the 12,000 foot pass of Bela-la , he bade us farewell and, according to custom, he and his men waved *katas* (white ceremonial scarves) and shouted farewell until we were out of sight.

The only thing that had marred the occasion was that we had just heard the sad news of the death of the Tulku of Gangten. He was only thirty years old and much liked and trusted by the Maharaja. We had planned to visit him at his seat of Tashi-chö-dzong in Thimpu. And although we passed within sight of that imposing building we did not enter it.

We now marched westwards towards Wangdü Photrang. On the first day we were plagued by flies. On day two we made a slight detour to visit Punakha, the old capital of Bhutan, where the dzong had been the scene of the installation of the present Maharaja in 1927. It was a picturesque place, situated on a tongue of land between two rivers, one of which, the Pho, was perfectly clear and designated male, while its neighbour, the Mo was rather dirty and said to be female! Both rivers were spanned by roofed bridges. The fine dzong possessed many large and small courtyards, in one of which we saw an orange tree in whose branches many pigeons were perched. The great hall, meanwhile, was about 130 feet square, and had gaily decorated columns and galleries. We climbed to the top of the tower and on our way down were shown a large room said to serve as a bathroom for the few lamas now inhabiting the place.

We halted for one day at Wangdü Photrang, which had a rather smaller dzong than the others we had seen, situated on a high bluff overlooking the junction of the Punakha river with a side stream. The altitude here was only about 4,500 feet above sea level, so it was rather hot.

That evening we were concerned to find that our dog, Bruce, was clearly out of sorts. Fearing that he might have pneumonia, he was wrapped in flannel and we fed him every four hours with brandy. To our great relief, he seemed much better in the morning. We travelled on for the next five days in the direction of Tongsa, encountering torrential rain on several occasions. It was then that I discovered the consolations of Bovril when one is cold and wet. Poor Derrick also got bitten by a leech. It had apparently fallen from a wayside branch and somehow managed to work its way underneath his watch. His arm later became swollen and very uncomfortable. Bruce, on the other hand, seemed to get better and better all the time, though he continued to be carried in his basket.

One stage out of Tongsa we were met by Dasho Gyurme Dorji, the Maharaja's brother, who gave us tea, saffron-rice, cheese and barley beer. He was a shy, sturdily built youth of twenty-two.

We first caught sight of Tongsa itself from about three miles off. Looking up the precipitous, densely wooded valley of the Tongsa Chu, the large white dzong with its round-towered outworks reared above us on its hillside. The two great Penlops of Bhutan are those of Paro and Tongsa. The Maharaja himself held the Tongsa title, having inherited it from his father; consequently he spent some weeks each year at the dzong there.

At Tongsa we were again lodged in a luxurious new guesthouse and, after lunch at the dzong, took part in an archery contest. Unfortunately, my first shot greatly amused the onlookers as it went high and stuck in a juniper tree. Then after dinner we tried our hand at the local dancing under the guidance of two of Tobgye's men. Only George Sherriff managed to master one of the steps completely, at the same time holding a hand-drum with its crescent-shaped stick.

After our day's halt at Tongsa, we proceeded towards Bumthang. A march and a half ahead, the Maharaja kindly send a *dandy* (carrying chair) ahead for me, a splendid vehicle with brocade upholstery, and eight equally splendidly attired *dandywallahs* to carry it. He also sent us dainty things to eat and drink: rice, jack-fruit, mangoes, *chang* (a Tibetan beer brewed from barley, which can be quite intoxicating), tea and cakes.

The next day we were met three miles from Bumthang by the Maharaja's youngest brother, Dasho Nako, a pleasant lad of fifteen who had brought with him a contingent of about thirty soldiers in mediaeval steel helmets, together with two dancers and a band. After refreshments, we proceeded in stately procession down a meandering hill to Bumthang itself, astride mules sent by the Maharaja. As we descended we caught sight in the distance of the mighty snow-capped mountains which we would have to cross in order to get into Tibet.

Outside Bumthang stood a guard of honour of about forty soldiers wearing khaki uniforms of locally woven material, Gurkha hats, belts and puttees, and carrying .303 rifles. All save the commander, who had been trained in Shillong with a Gurkha regiment, were barefoot. Thus, preceded by dancers and soldiers, we completed the last half mile of our journey, passing the Maharaja's house and arriving at the camp and guest-houses, the only permanent buildings in Bumthang, it seemed, which was really more of a summer camp than a settled capital. At the gate of the camp, we had the honour of being met by the Maharaja himself, who was then about twenty-nine and very good looking. He was wearing a handsome striped silk chuba and embroidered boots with pointed toes. We all went inside the guest-house, were offered tea, saffron-rice and fruit, talked a little, and then the Maharaja's two brothers, Dasho Gyurme Dorji and Dasho Nako, tactfully withdrew so that official matters could be discussed.

After lunch we were visited by the ladies of His Highness's family, all of whom were beautifully dressed in rich brocade jackets and Bhutanese dresses, earrings, beads, bracelets and rings. They wore no stockings—just white tennis shoes on their feet. The Maharani had a lovely profile and a thoroughly nice nature to go with it. She was then about twenty-three and the mother of Jigme, the heir apparent, a vivacious child of five, who had not a trace of shyness. The Maharani and the other royal ladies stayed to tea and then returned with the Maharaja and his two brothers for dinner. There were fifteen of us that night and, what with a cinema show after dinner and then games like Grunt, Piggy, Grunt! and Up Jenkins!, we didn't get to bed until well after eleven o'clock.

There was, of course, a formal side to our visit to Bumthang. Derrick called upon His Highness the Maharaja in full dress uniform and then the Maharaja duly returned the call wearing hid KCIE (Knight Commander of the Most Eminent Order of the Indian Empire) and a gold Bhutanese medal. In addition, they had a number of official meetings when they discussed such matters as the financial needs of Bhutan and the vexed question of Darchin, the small monastery at the foot of the sacred Mount Kailas in western Tibet, where there had recently been trouble. Darchin had traditionally been administered by the Bhutanese but lately the Tibetan authorities had begun to encroach upon their rights there. Derrick had visited Darchin with Lud in 1932 during their brief tour of western Tibet, and he was later again able to take up the matter with the Tibetan Government in Lhasa. Finally, His Highness expressed a strong desire to visit Calcutta during the cold season of 1934.

I got on very well with the ladies of the royal household. Besides the Maharani, there was Aji Pedon, who was about fifty, a delightful person. She was the half-sister of the Maharaja and mother to the Paro Penlop. Aji Wangmo was the Maharaja's younger sister, a plump and jolly young woman of nineteen.

Just before dinner one evening the Maharani dressed me up in the finest Bhutanese costume, complete with small pillbox hat of vivid colours and all the jewellery. I looked enormously stout. I then dressed Her Highness up in some of my own clothes: dress, hat, stockings, shoes. She was very pleased, though she must have felt the cold as my clothes were much flimsier than hers.

On the last day of our stay, five coolies appeared loaded with presents for us from the Maharaja and his family. There were beautiful hand-woven materials, baskets, boxes and also a set of Bhutanese costumes for Derrick as well as another for myself. His Highness and his family then came to lunch. His Highness looked splendid in all his medals and a round hat topped with a small peacock's head. They all came back to dinner and after more games we finished up singing 'Auld Lang Syne' together.

We left Bumthang on 27 July, with both traditional and modern soldiers marching ahead. We were accompanied for the first half mile by the royal ladies; Derrick and Aji Pedon in front, the Maharani, myself and Aji Wangmo following, all of us holding hands. When at last it was time to say goodbye, we exchanged katas. Then Derrick was presented with a silver cigarette box and I with three gold rings studded with turquoises, all the work of the royal craftsmen. Our gracious hosts seemed genuinely sorry to see us go – and I was certainly sad to leave them.

Later that day there were two mishaps. First I fell from the new pony which the Maharaja had given us. Then later five *syces* (grooms) fell into a stream, together with their horses when a rotten wooden bridge gave way beneath them. Happily no human or horse was seriously hurt and we all arrived safely at our campsite at Shapjetang, where the Maharaja and his brothers were waiting to greet us.

Next day had been reserved for shikar. All the men went out looking for wild pig, except for Dasho Gyurme Dorji, who was out of sorts. I meanwhile remained in camp to wash my hair—and amused the coolies when I tried to dry it in the sun.

When we said goodbye to the Maharaja's brothers next morning we were worried by the fact that Dasho Gyurme Dorji had been and was still very feverish. We became even more concerned when we later heard that he had typhoid. A young Bhutanese doctor who had been trained in India did all he could to save his life, but his efforts were hindered by the local lamas, who hold very different views from our own in medical matters and whose influence in Bhutan was then exceedingly strong. Gyurme Dorji in fact died in September. An intelligent and attractive young man with a pronounced sense of service, this was a great loss to his country. Derrick and I also felt it as a personal loss.

About two miles further along a wet, stony path we came to a reception tent erected in our honour by the Maharaja. He invited us inside for tea and saffron-rice, and then we took leave of each other. We exchanged katas and as a parting gift His Highness gave us a set of small ivory bowls lined with silver. Then we mounted and rode away, waving katas and calling until we could see the Maharaja no more.

Now we began to climb in earnest towards the crest of the main Himalayan range in order to cross into Tibet. The coniferous trees that until now had crowded the lower hillsides became thinner, giving way eventually to rhododendrons and alpine flowers, while above we could see bare, rocky ridges. Then on 29 July, shortly after we had taken leave of our friend Tobgye, the landscape became more rugged as we travelled up a stony plain bounded on either side by great mountains.

We reached a glacial river about forty yards wide, which we had to cross by jumping from one stone to another. Unfortunately one of the ponies lost its footing and became lodged between rocks. The coolies tried unsuccessfully to release it for about twenty minutes, the poor creature getting colder and colder in the glacial water. At last they managed to manoeuvre it onto a rock and then tied its front and back legs together so that they could lift and drag it over to the far bank. Derrick found a bottle of whisky and poured half of the contents down the poor pony's throat, which seemed to have a magical effect, and he was soon fully recovered. We hoped he wouldn't develop a craving for the stuff!

We made a cold, windy camp that night, our last in Bhutan. A little rain fell and gradually mist enveloped us. After a day's halt, we set off at seven a.m. Though distinctly chilly, the sky had cleared and it was a marvellous morning. Having passed a moraine and the Tsogyu lake, we exchanged our ponies for sure-footed yaks, which were better suited to high-altitude travelling. Mine was a nice, brown, silken-haired animal. We climbed higher and higher until we reached the foot of the glacier. On the way we passed more lakes and also saw some *bharal* (wild blue sheep).

It was hard going even for yak over the ice, but in two and a half hours we reached the Mon-la Kar Chung pass. Just short of the top, however, our way was barred by an ominous crevasse, but using planks thoughtfully sent by His Highness we were able to get across it safely.

The view from the top was absolutely stunning. Gigantic crags including the 24,784 foot Kula Kangri reared up on all sides, with the snow and ice on their knife-edged ridges glistening brilliantly in the crisp morning sunshine. Derrick and I stood there, utterly amazed at the sublime beauty and grandeur of the Himalayas. Beautiful as it was, however, that remote and lofty pass was not a place in which to linger long. Behind us lay the green, idyllic land of Bhutan, home of many new-found friends; ahead lay the mysterious 'forbidden land' of Tibet, and we were both eager to move on.

5 The Road to Lhasa

In Bhutan Derrick and I had become used to travelling through a landscape of green, wooded hills and deep valleys. Here in Tibet, however, what we encountered were bare, brown hills, arid and devoid of vegetation, with occasional snow peaks looming above them. It was a stark, almost primeval landscape, yet strangely beautiful. Colours were particularly striking. They reached the eye with vivid intensity because the air at that altitude was so thin and clear that there was nothing in the atmosphere to filter down impressions. For the same reason, distant objects appeared nearer than they in fact were. A building, for instance, might seem just an hour's travelling time ahead, but after that hour it might still seem just as far away. Overhead, meanwhile, the sky was a deep, deep blue in which floated fleecy white clouds. All in all, it wasn't so much like crossing from one geographical zone to another as being translated into an entirely different world. Tibet really was unlike anywhere else.

Having descended from the frontier pass, we were met by the dzongpön of Towa Dzong, a pleasant young man who offered us chang. The dzongpön had been detailed by the Tibetan Government to accompany us all the way to Lhasa and look after the arrangements for our transport and supplies.

As in Bhutan, we travelled mainly in the mornings, endeavouring to be off to a good start and to make each day's camp around midday as in the afternoons a strong wind often blew up. We were not travelling by the usual route to Lhasa. That lay further to the west, straight down from the Natu-la to Yatung in the Chumbi Valley and on by way of Phari and Gyantse. We planned to connect up with it at Nagartse, which was situated beyond Gyantse, but in the meantime we moved along unfrequented byways.

OUR FIRST CAMPSITE in Tibet was at Longdo, a hamlet consisting of a single house only. In the afternoon the sun was very hot but, after it had gone down, a bitter wind began to blow. Thus were we summarily introduced to the extremes of heat and cold that so often prevail in Tibet. There were no trees to lend us any shelter and one or two of our servants had to be given treatment for snowblindness, having refused to wear snowglasses while crossing the glacier.

Next morning it was pleasantly warm again as we followed the Longdo river eastwards. White-crested peaks of the main Himalayan range emerged behind the nearer hills as we travelled. We arrived shortly after midday at Se, a small village that possessed a monastery said to have been built singlehandedly by the great eleventh-century Tibetan mystic, Milarepa, of whom the Tibetans are particularly fond. There are many stories about him, including one that tells how at one point in his life, whilst meditating in the mountains, he existed exclusively on nettles, a diet that lent his body the greenish tinge which often appears on Tibetan *thangkas*, or scroll paintings, of him. He was also a great poet and singer.

From Se, we travelled northwards to the rich and well-cultivated Lhobrak valley, were we saw fine crops of barley, mustard, peas and some wheat. The valley was flanked on either side by bare and rugged mountains that rose up against a rich blue sky in which many white clouds floated. The Tibetan houses that we passed were of the same basic design, being flat roofed and squarely built around a central courtyard. Nearly all had clumps of willow or poplar growing around them.

Shortly after 1.30 pm on 3 August, we made camp in a willow grove at Towa Dzong. The dzong itself and the local monastery were perched on the summit of a sheer five-hundred foot cliff, while near by there was one of those long *mani-walls* that are so characteristic of Tibet. These walls are composed of rough stone tablets on which the faithful have carved *mantras*. The favourite is 'Om Mani Padme Hum', the mantra of Chenrezig, the Buddha of compassion, which one saw and heard everywhere. We also found many brightly-coloured flowers in the vicinity and collected specimens of a bright blue delphinium for Ludlow and Sherriff. Our transport arrived some time after we had got into camp ourselves. Yaks travel with great steadiness and sureness, but very slowly; a good average rate for them is about two miles an hour.

We halted the next day at Towa Dzong to visit the dzong and to take lunch with the local dzongpön and his wife, who was a very charming but shy lady. During our guided tour they showed us the prison cells, in which there were a set of primitive stocks and a deep hole into which, apparently, prisoners used to be thrown. I had heard gossip about the Draconian punishments said to be meted out in Tibet at that time, although throughout our whole time in the country we saw very few instances. Derrick assured me that all the reports that he had read indicated that the incidence of crime was very low and that the harshest punishments were reserved for those who had committed serious political offences.

We later went back to our camp, where the dzongpön and his wife returned our call and stayed to tea. Both took advantage of the opportunity to get vaccinated against smallpox by Captain Tennant. Although in general the Tibetans held very different views in medical matters to ours, by the 1930s the value of vaccination was appreciated and encouraged by the Tibetan Government. In all, Tennant gave some 1,340 vaccinations during our tour of Tibet that year.

On the morning of 5 August, we rode up a dramatic sandstone gorge, sheer cliffs walling us in on either hand. Then we climbed to the Uyu-la, a 16,150 foot pass that possessed two crests about half a mile apart. We were surprised to find grazing up there herds of yak, which chased our dog, Bruce, perhaps taking him for a wolf, of which there were said to be plenty in the region.

Fortunately, we did not encounter any wolves but we did see marmot and, later wild sheep. There was no question of having any sport, however, as we were too close to the holy city of Lhasa. As in Bhutan, the prevailing outlook of the people made them frown upon all forms of shikar, and indeed on cruelty to animals of any sort. Buddhists place great emphasis on the sanctity of life and they try to avoid activities that directly or indirectly cause suffering. As a consequence, many of the wild animals we encountered during our tours of Tibet, having never been subject to attack by humans, were amazingly tame and did not necessarily take instant flight upon seeing us as would certainly have happened elsewhere. The same desire not to cause unnecessary suffering applied to the Tibetans' treatment of domesticated animals. I don't remember seeing a dog or a beast of burden being beaten or abused in any way by adult or child. Of course, Derrick, with his great love of shikar, felt a certain frustration at having to pass so much tempting quarry by, but he knew how the Tibetans felt in these matters and would not for a moment have dreamt of offending them.

From the double pass of Uyu-la, we dropped down into a broad, open valley that drained into the great lake of Yam-drok Tso. We camped there that day and shortly after we had found our site, a bleak spot, the heavens darkened and a great hail-and thunderstorm broke and raged for half an hour. It was very localized, however, and the ground was white only for about a mile around our camp. At 15,600 feet, this was our highest camp and, being above the tree-line, all our cooking had to be done over acrid yak-dung fires, as is very often the case in the largely treeless wastes of Tibet. That night, the sky was beautifully clear and the stars shone brilliantly.

The following day we rode into a broad plain in which meandered the Kurkyum river. Here we were formally met by a recruiting officer who had his headquarters in the adjacent community of Ling. Despite the fact that he worked for the Tibetan Army, this man was an ordained monk. He wore full official robes of yellow and cinnamon-brown silk and, on his head, a round hat of yellow papier mâché. After formal greetings, he courteously escorted us to a rather grand Tibetan tent that had been set up in our honour, where we were given lunch. Afterwards we were presented with newly killed sheep, eggs and Tibetan cloth.

Having taken our leave of this kindly monastic recruiting officer, we proceeded on our way. After about half a mile we rounded a bend and saw before us a magnificent panorama of snow mountains, with low, bare hills below them and, at their foot, the great lake of Yamdrok Tso itself, a vast sheet of water perfectly mirroring the vivid blue of the sky.

Travelling along the shores of the lake the next morning, we saw numerous bar-headed geese, brahminy duck and mallard; also groups of gazelle, which were so tame that we could approach to within fifty yards of them.

After lunch, we went on to the village of Talung, which as its name suggests—it means 'horse country'—is famous throughout Tibet for its horses. Every year in August a great horse fair is held there. We found the place to be of the usual Tibetan pattern: a high rock crowned with a dzong and the village clustered around the base. As we rode in, the inhabitants came rushing out excitedly to see us and then gawped unashamedly as we proceeded to pitch camp, clearly as much fascinated by our equipment as by ourselves. There can often be something threatening about crowds, even small ones. But not that day at Talung. The people seemed so good-hearted and innocent that, though at first I was a little taken aback to be the object of their enthusiastic attention, I was soon won round by their happy smiles and gay laughter. That afternoon I watched bricks being made just in front of our camp—and a gang of completely naked children had a wonderful time playing in the mud in the warm afternoon sunshine.

Next day, 8 August, we followed the western shores of the Yamdrok Tso, though periodically we had to leave them in order to negotiate high passes. We passed Samding monastery, where the abbess is the only female tulku in Tibet, Dorje Phagmo, literally 'Thunderbolt Sow.'

Apparently the legend runs that in the early eighteenth century a horde of nominally Buddhist Mongols bore down upon the monastery. Their chief sent orders ahead to the Dorje Phagmo of the day to present herself and show whether or not it was true that she possessed a sow's head. She refused, which infuriated the chieftain. He tore down the monastery walls and broke into Dorje Phagmo's sanctuary, to find the place devoid of human beings; the only occupants were a litter of pigs presided over by a gigantic sow! Dumbstruck, the Mongol chief gave up any plan of sacking the monastery, whereupon all the pigs turned back into nuns and monks and the sow into Dorje Phagmo. The Mongols heaped gifts on the monastery before taking flight.

Apparently the present Dorje Phagmo's sister had just died and so we postponed our visit until another time.

Our route joined the main Gyantse–Lhasa road at Nagartse, a small village with the obligatory dzong, where we paused for a whole day. The morning was passed lazily in writing letters; then the lay dzongpön came to lunch with his wife. As was the case with many offices in Tibet, there was also a monk dzongpön, but he did not put in an appearance. We were altogether twelve at that meal, including Rai Sahib Bo, the Sikkimese doctor from the Agency at Gyantse, who had joined our party to assist Captain Tennant. We ate out in the sun and Samdup, Derrick's factotum, played the gramophone.

In the afternoon, we visited Nagartse dzong, where we saw the throne of the Great Fifth Dalai Lama, and also what was said to be his footprint in the rock. The Fifth Dalai Lama, who lived in the seventeenth century, was a strong and wise ruler. With great political acumen, he skilfully played off the Mongols against the Manchu Emperor of China to unite and strengthen Tibet. It was he who consolidated spiritual and temporal power in the office of the Dalai Lama, and he also initiated the method of selecting Panchen Lamas based on the principle of reincarnation. A great patron of learning and the religious arts, the Potala as we know it was largely built under his guiding hand.

According to custom, we left presents for both dzongpöns and afterwards made our way back to camp from the dzong, calling in at the local telegraph office to speak to Mr. Worth, the current BTA at Gyantse. In a way it was good to feel back in touch with the world after all our wanderings in the wilds of Bhutan and southern Tibet. The first telegraph line linking Tibet with India was constructed as far as Gyantse by the Younghusband Expedition. Such a flimsy metal thread could have been easily severed by the Tibetans, cutting off rapid communications between the Expedition's leaders and their superior officers in India. The Tibetans did not do this, however, and the explanation usually given is that they thought the line to be a kind of 'Ariadne's thread' that was to help the British intruders find their way back out of Tibet once their business was done. To have cut that vital link might have meant to have these unwanted guests on their hands indefinitely. Later they came to appreciate the usefulness of the telegraph and in 1923 Mr. King of the Telegraph Department of Bengal continued the line from Gyantse to Lhasa itself. Sir Charles Bell, who had been instrumental in obtaining the technical help for this project, was the recipient of one of the first, perhaps the very first, cable sent from Lhasa, which reached him in Banff in Scotland shortly after his retirement. British officers stationed at Phari looked after the line, notably Mr. Rosemeyer, whose duties took him frequently to the holy city.

Although violent thunderstorms raged all night, they had abated by the time we set off next day. We then left the Yamdrok Tso and climbed towards the 16,000 foot Nyapso-la, on the way passing a stone wall built by the Tibetans in 1904 in an unsuccessful effort to frustrate the advance of Colonel Younghusband's force. From the head of the Nyapso-la we got a magnificent view: the endless mountains were suddenly interrupted by the well-cultivated valley of the mighty Tsangpo river. Rising in western Tibet, a little to the east of the sacred Kailas mountain and Lake Manasa-rovar, the Tsangpo is one of the great arteries of southern Asia. Having traversed southern Tibet, it eventually turns south and, breaking through the formidable Himalayan mountain barrier, becomes the Brahmaputra that flows through Assam. Standing up there on the Nyapso-la, sweep-ing the landscape with field-glasses, it was almost unbeliev-able that this massive body of water should flow through such an arid landscape. We could see tiny coracles moored to trees near the middle of the river; and on the near shore, in a pleasant willow grove among barley fields, the day's camp being prepared for us. Derrick suggested we drift down the river in these coracles instead of crossing by ferry, a suggestion to which I readily agreed.

The way down into the Tsangpo valley from the pass was exceedingly steep and we had to get off our ponies and walk in places. On the way we passed a dak house where runners bearing the official mail were changed. We often saw these mail-runners, who usually carried packs upon their backs and what looked like jesters' wands, with bells on the end which tinkled as they ran along.

Kanchung, where we camped that day, was a pleasant spot, if rather hot. As we were making camp the local headman turned up bearing gifts of food. The Tibetan Government obliged local officials to provide authorized travellers with supplies, and also with lodging and transport, if required. It was a form of taxation. On the other hand, it was strictly illegal to furnish any help whatsoever to unauthorized travel-lers, thus making it virtually impossible for anyone not bearing the government's permit to travel in the country. This was a primary way in which the policy of seclusion was maintained, and it was highly effective, as one realizes if one reads the accounts of such people as Alexandra David-Néel and the eccentric British Buddhist Montgomery McGovern, both of whom suffered great hardships when they tried to travel illegally in Tibet.

As I rose the following morning, I felt very excited at the prospect of encountering the great river. It had rained heavily all night but the sky had cleared by the time we reached the Cabra ferry. Here we were held up for some time as part of our kit was loaded into yak-skin coracles and ferried across. The ponies were also taken across; they were tied to the coracles and had to swim for it. Derrick had his Leica and was photographing our preparations. He was worried, though, that our plan to go by river would be foiled. The Tibetans are great ones for precedent and, it seemed, no Political Officer had gone down the river before. And if anything happened, it would be the responsibility of the local chieftain.

But no objection was raised to our plan, perhaps because the river was running low and was less dangerous than usual. Eventually our coracles were brought up and we got on board. They were primitive craft, each made of about four yak skins sewn together with stout thongs and stretched over a sturdy willow frame; they were steered by a paddle at the rear. Derrick and I got into one, along with Samdup, Bruce and a boatman. The other members of our party got into a second one, which was roped to ours, except for Norbhu and Tennant who preferred to be taken across by the regular ferry and to ride down to Chushul.

It was very pleasant to drift down the river and enjoy the passing scenery. We sat on *yakdans* (wooden packing cases) and the current moved us along quite quickly. About four miles before we reached Chushul, we passed the great iron bridge at Chaksam, where a *gompa* (chapel) overlooked the river from a gaunt hillside. No one knew precisely how long the bridge had been there but, at the time we went by, it reached only as far as an island about a quarter of the way across. Near by, flat wooden ferry-boats were moored. These, which had crude horses' heads fixed to their prows rather in the manner of ancient Viking ships, were used to take people across when the river was running low.

Having passed a number of villages lying in pleasant willow groves on the banks, we arrived at Chushul, where we found other coracles being unloaded onto a stony spit. A rocky spur ran directly down to the spit from a ruined dzong perched on an eminence higher up. We camped that day in a willow grove beyond Chushul and I noted in my diary that the trees thereabouts all seemed to have been pollarded and thereby made to look rather like fat palm trunks with crops of whippy suckers jutting out of their tops.

Next day our road ran right alongside the Kyi Chu for much of its distance and in one place had been blasted out some years before to allow the passage of a pair of elephants that the Maharaja of Nepal was sending as presents to the Dalai Lama.

THERE WAS NOW MUCH EXCITEMENT in the air for Lhasa was very near — and Lhasa was not just the capital of Tibet: it was a holy city, venerated by Buddhists across the length and breadth of Central Asia. From distant Mongolia, Siberia, China and Russian Turkestan, as well as through the entire Himalayan region from west to east, pilgrim routes converged upon this sacred place, and down them the faithful travelled, negligent of hardship and privation, in order to place their offerings upon the city's legendary shrines. Indeed we ourselves were travelling upon such a route and met with a number of pilgrims, rosary and prayer-wheel in hand, murmuring mantras. Some pilgrims prostrated the whole length of their journey, often taking years to reach Lhasa.

Apart from its great spiritual significance, Lhasa had acquired a special mystique for Westerners because it had always been closed to outsiders. Derrick's study at the Residency at Gangtok was lined with books in which intrepid nineteenth- and early twentieth-century travellers described their abortive attempts to enter the forbidden city. The Younghusband Expedition had allowed many Indian Army officers and men to lift the veil and behold the mysteries of Lhasa, but only three Western women had preceded me there.

Eight miles from our campsite on the day before our arrival at Lhasa, we were met by the first of the many official reception committees sent ahead to welcome us by the Tibetan Government. This one was headed by Tampa Tsedron, a monk, who presented Derrick and me with a kata. He told us that he was to be one of our two guides while we were in Lhasa. The other would be Changlochen Kusho, lately appointed one of the Dalai Lama's *garpöns* or viceroys in western Tibet, though apparently he had no intention of exchanging the sophistication of life in the capital for bleak exile in the wastes of Ngari Khorsum and had dispatched a proxy to discharge his duties there.

Our campsite that day was in a *lingka* or walled garden. Rough grass and a few poplars grew there, but there was not enough space for more than just one tent, so the servants and the clerks had to pitch theirs outside, along with the kitchen tent. We got off to a good start just after eight o'clock the following morning. After about six miles the road began to ascend steeply. Derrick urged his pony forward, moving steadily ahead of me. At the brow of the incline, he reined in his mount and, shading his eyes with his hand, scanned the horizon. The holy city was in sight.

6   New Friends in Lhasa

LHASA WAS STILL more than ten miles away and very small in the distance, but the sight of the morning sunshine glittering on the golden roofs of the Potala took my breath away. We could also see Chakpori, the medical college, which, like the Potala, is one of those imposing Tibetan buildings built on the top of a hill that seem to grow out of the rock itself.

We moved on to the Trisam ferry, where we found a fine Tibetan tent pitched and chang prepared for us. There should have been a bridge there but it had been swept away by floods the month before. While we paused for rest and refreshment, the transport animals were unloaded and sent swimming across the river. Later, having taken photographs, we followed in yak-skin boats.

On the far bank, the Tibetan members of our party began to don their best official dress, for we were now very near the holy city. We were escorted onwards by one of the Dalai Lama's lay guides, who had been sent out to meet us, and our Tibetan monk guide, who wore a flat, round, hat with a wide brim of a rich golden colour. After about a mile we met Rai Sahib Bo, who was returning from Lhasa whence he had been sent the day before by Derrick to present the Dalai Lama and his government with katas on our behalf. He had now with him two of his relations and a number of Ladakhi Mussulman (Moslem) traders, who, as citizens of India, enjoyed the benefits of British protection.

On a rocky hillside to our left rose, tier upon tier, the numerous flat-roofed, whitewashed buildings of the great

Drepung monastery, an awe-inspiring sight. This massive complex, I was told, housed 7,700 monks, though often far more than that were actually in residence—perhaps even at times as many as 10,000, which made it the largest monastery in the world.

A little below Drepung and to the right was the house of Nechung Oracle, who was the State Oracle and believed to be able to predict future events.

Once a year this monk is brought out with great pomp and ceremony to be possessed by a deity. He is carefully prepared for this for some time beforehand, living in seclusion, meditating and eating only the purest foods. When the great occasion comes he is dressed in elaborate and highly colourful robes of Chinese brocade, and a tall hat, golden and beplumed, is tied onto his head. Then, as the monks chant and play music on long horns, gyelings, cymbals and drums, he begins to go into trance. Gradually the deity takes over his body; he begins to shudder; every muscle and sinew is under such pressure that they stand out like cords. Then, suddenly, he will leap up and do a wild, whirling dance. Finally he begins to utter his prophecies in a strange, high-pitched voice. He predicts what will befall the Dalai Lama, the Tibetan people and the Tibetan Government during the forthcoming year.

Three miles from Lhasa, we were met by the reception committees. First we were greeted by the Bhutanese Agent and the representatives of the Nepalese Agent in Lhasa. Then, a mile further on, along a stretch of road bounded by marshland where waterlilies grew in profusion, we came to a small garden in which a grand Tibetan pavilion had been pitched. Here a number of officials were waiting to present us with more katas and to serve us tea and rice on behalf of the Dalai Lama and his Government. I was astonished at the enormous size of the great silver and gilt teapots that were used.

After a short halt, we continued for about 500 yards before coming to the Norbhu Lingka, the summer palace of the

Dalai Lama, a long, imposing building set amid lovely gardens. Here about four hundred soldiers were drawn up as a guard of honour. They were commanded by Depön Shasur and four *gyapöns* (literally, 'commander of a hundred'), and had with them a brass band that played creditably. Colours were also carried. The soldiers all wore khaki drill uniforms—not the smartest—and trousers, but no puttees. A few had western-style boots but most had on the colourful high Tibetan cloth boots with rope or leather soles. They carried .303 rifles which the British had supplied. While Derrick went off with Bruce to inspect them, the crowd surged around me, fairly bubbling over with curiosity. As they all seemed so good-natured, I felt perfectly at home among them.

'Their drill was pretty good,' Derrick told me when he had got back from his inspection. 'Some of those chaps have just got back from fighting the Chinese in Kham. And fine, strapping chaps they are too. I'm impressed!'

As we continued our progress towards the holy city, the imposing bulk of the Potala loomed nearer and larger all the time. We turned our ponies to the right and rode down a lane with high walls enclosing lingkas on either side until we came to a broad highway about forty yards wide. This was the motor route along which the Dalai Lama was driven when he went from the Potala to the Norbhu Lingka, or vice versa.

Finally, turning down yet another lane, we came at last to the gates of Dekyi Lingka, literally the 'Garden of Happiness'—an auspicious name for a place that was to be our home for the next seven weeks. We rode along for about five minutes beside the stream that ran through the garden and passed the extensive outbuildings which were to house our hospital and offices. Then we came to another gate in the wall encircling the house itself and its inner garden. Here we were greeted by our lay guide, Changlochen Kusho.

All the British missions to Lhasa, from that of Sir Charles Bell onwards, were accommodated in Dekyi Lingka, which was the property of the Abbot of Kundeling monastery. The house itself was a typical square, flat-roofed Tibetan building of two storeys, built around a courtyard, with ancillary buildings including stables, kitchens and servants' quarters. Captain Tennant was quartered on the ground floor, where there was also a large dining-hall with many colourfully painted pillars. This room was large enough for receptions. A steep and somewhat rickety Tibetan staircase led up to the first floor, on one side of which was a comfortable red-pillared sitting-room. The furnishings here included numerous *bodens* (hard, square or oblong cushions) and fine old Khotan carpets. This room opened out onto a very pleasant balcony, and next door there was an office in which Derrick could work. On the other side of the landing there were three rooms which we used as bedroom, dressing-room and bathroom.

The principal drawback of the Dekyi Lingka at that time was that it had no glass in the windows, just pieces of gauze on wooden frames which had to be inserted at night in order to keep out the cold air and taken out in the day to let in the light and the fresh air. Fortunately our visit was taking place in summer, but clearly in winter the house would be bitterly cold. Being summer we also had the great pleasure of being able to see the profusion of bright salmon-coloured holly-hocks which grew in the garden and the peach, walnut and poplar trees.

Having seen over the house, we went back downstairs to the dining-room, where the Tibetan Government had most hospitably laid on tea, chang and a very good Tibetan lunch for us. How nice it was to have a settled base again, even though a temporary one, after having been almost constantly on the move for ten weeks.

WE WERE DUE TO HAVE AN AUDIENCE with His Holiness the Dalai Lama on the third day after our arrival. His Holiness, Thubten Gyatso, popularly known as the 'Great Thirteenth' on account of his powerful personality and considerable achievements, had been born in 1876 of peasant stock at the village of Perchöde in Thakpo Langdun in south-eastern Tibet, exactly where the Nechung Oracle had predicted.

The Potala.

The entrance to Lhasa.

(Previous page) His Holiness the Thirteenth Dalai Lama.

The Prime Minister of Tibet.

Kunphel-la with TIBET No. 2.

Tea cauldron and police sentry box near the Jokhang.

Lhasa street scene.

Mint machinery at Trapchi.

The railway at Trapchi.

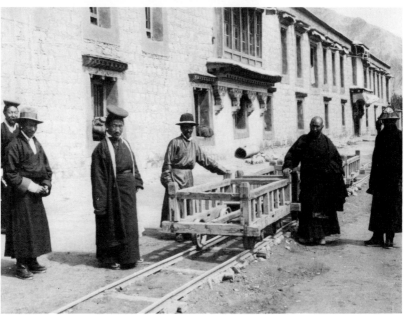

Parade at Trapchi.

Self with ladies of the Tsarong house.

The ladies party at Dekyi Lingka.

Lungshar and family.

Children's party.

Ringang with his family.

*At Dekyi Lingka.
Standing: Tsarong
Dzasa, Jigme Taring,
Derrick, Norbhu. Seated:
Mrs Tsarong, self, Mary
Taring and Dundul.*

After his formal enthronement in 1879 the Dalai Lama was given a rigorous education, learning the Buddhist scriptures by heart, reciting them and studying them in depth with his tutors. He also took various monastic vows and received major and minor initiations. 'I studied every day without fail to the best of my intellectual capacity,' he wrote in his final testament.

At eighteen years of age, his inexperience notwithstanding, His Holiness assumed full temporal and religious power, afterwards dedicating himself wholeheartedly to the advancement of Buddhism, to the strengthening of the political system in Tibet and the general well-being of his people. He had to steer his country through turbulent times when both foreign powers and various aspects of the modern world, many of them totally inimical to the traditional lifestyle of Tibet, began to impinge upon that country. Yet he was fully willing to embrace the challenge and became one of the most effective of the Dalai Lamas. As Sir Charles Bell has recorded, his capacity for work was prodigious. During the time of Bell's visit to Lhasa in 1920–21, he was rising at around six a.m., earlier if occasion demanded it, and continuing through the day, interspersing religious and secular duties until past midnight. Bell believed that it was this rigorous regime, coupled with the stress inevitably produced by a fiery temperament—though admittedly the passing years did temper the impetuosity of his youth—that gradually undermined his health. He in fact fell ill while Bell was in the holy city and, by the early 1930s, when well into his fifties and old by the Tibetan standards of the day, his health had further deteriorated. So much so that in 1932 an additional Mönlam Chenmo ('Great Prayer Festival') was held in Lhasa, during which the Nechung Oracle advised the people both to beg His Holiness to prolong his present sojourn in the world and to beg his pardon for their various sins and omissions. A little later the Tibetan Government ordered the performance of a special ceremony called Tenshug ('Plea for Eternal Stay') and a general appeal was submitted.

In the field of foreign affairs, His Holiness had to deal with his powerful neighbours in China and British India, both of whom invaded his kingdom during his reign, thereby forcing him into exile. But he survived both exiles and invasions, and indeed in 1913, when he returned in triumph to his capital after the invading Chinese army had been driven out, he was determined to establish the independence of his country. He in no way recognized Chinese claims to any kind of authority over Tibet, nor did he wish to have their troops or officials stationed on Tibetan soil. At the same time, however, he had no wish to be at odds with the Chinese. His Holiness also wished to be on good terms with the British in India, not least because they could provide him with help that was essential if the independence of Tibet was to be anything more than an illusion. The essence of His Holiness's foreign policy was therefore to balance Tibet, which was a militarily weak country, between China on the one hand and British India on the other, both of which possessed powerful armies.

Having returned to Tibet, His Holiness was aware of the fact that if Tibetan independence was to be a reality he would have to introduce some modern innovations. In particular, an army equipped with modern weapons and trained in their use was required. Also he wished to develop the natural resources of Tibet (for instance, by opening up new mineral mining operations), as well as introducing electricity, telegraphy, a police force in the capital and Western education. In all these endeavours he unfortunately tried to proceed too far too quickly and ran into much resistance from the conservatives.

AT LAST THE DAY OF OUR AUDIENCE with His Holiness dawned. We were up early and set off soon after nine in the morning, riding along the broad road that ran towards the Norbhu Lingka. It had been very wet in Lhasa that year and the ground on either side, where willows and poplars grew in profusion, was waterlogged.

Derrick had to prepare himself inwardly for the audience, for Tibetan society of that day was very formal and everything had to be done according to time-honoured custom. He looked rather special in his full dress uniform, with cocked hat, ceremonial sword and lots of gold braid. Captain Tennant was also in uniform, and Rai Bahadur Norbhu wore the full robes of a Tibetan official of the fourth rank: a yellow silk chuba caught up at the waist with a silk sash from which, at the rear, a pair of chopsticks hung, and on his head a wide-brimmed hat with red fringes around the crown, ribbons and various honorific ornaments of precious stones. I myself, out of respect, wore a long-skirted suit of French tweed and a felt hat.

The Norbhu Lingka was surrounded by a high stone wall pierced by various gates at which guards were stationed. We entered by the fourth gate and were immediately greeted by three officers and a guard who ushered us into a courtyard with a floor of crazy-paving. An abundance of hollyhocks grew here and over against the house there were more pots containing marigolds, nasturtiums and pinks. The Tibetans grow flowers in pots so that they can be taken indoors during the colder seasons of the year. As I admired them, suddenly a huge monk—a veritable giant—bore down upon us. He must have been at least seven feet tall and had some kind of board beneath his robes to make his broad shoulders look even broader. I learnt later that he was a *simgakpa*, or doorkeeper. He bowed ceremonially and, motioning us to follow, led us through an ante-room and into a small public reception room where the Dalai Lama was waiting to greet us. More flowers in pots stood all around on the highly polished floor.

His Holiness was seated on a raised dais about three steps high that rested upon brass lions. His head was shaven in accordance with monastic custom, his cheeks were full and his ears large—it was really a powerful peasant's head endowed with a strange elfin quality. His robes were sumptuous, made of the finest Chinese brocades, intricately decorated, with long sleeves from which the ends of his fingers could be seen protruding. His Tibetan boots were of black leather embroidered with green thread.

In attendance were the Dalai Lama's two favourites;

Kusho Kunphel-la and Tashi Dhondup. Kunphel-la was a tall, good-looking monk of about twenty-eight. Next to the Dalai Lama himself, he was undoubtedly the most powerful person in Tibet at the time. He held no official rank but constantly attended His Holiness, who in fact treated him like a son. Of high intelligence, he was the sort of man whose undoubted talents would inevitably bring him to the fore anywhere. However, I found out later that his talents caused jealousy and he had many enemies in the intrigue-ridden world of Lhasa politics. Also in attendance was Kusho R.D. Ringang, one of the boys who had been sent to Rugby School, who acted as interpreter for me. Derrick was able to speak directly with His Holiness in Tibetan.

Derrick entered the room first. He exchanged katas and shook hands with His Holiness. I did the same, followed by Captain Tennant. We all sat down on chairs at right angles to the throne and almost on the same level as His Holiness—a mark of the esteem in which we were held as representatives of the British Government. Finally Rai Bahadur Norbhu came in, took off his hat and prostrated three times, offered a kata and finally went forward to receive a blessing in the form of a simple touch on the head.

Next came the presentation of our gifts, which included seven service rifles, twelve hundred rounds of ammunition, four silver dishes and two mechanical lamps. Afterwards, a servant brought us Indian tea and Jacob's Golden Puff biscuits, while Kunphel-la served the Dalai Lama with Tibetan tea, which he drank from a gold tea cup.

Once social proceedings got under way, His Holiness was very warm and friendly and smiled a great deal. In an unusually low, guttural bass voice, he asked Derrick various questions. Were His Majesty the King-Emperor and the Viceroy in good health? Were we in good health ourselves? Had we had a good journey? The only thing that seemed to upset him was that we had sailed down the Tsangpo in a yak-skin coracle.

'Oh, but you should not have done this,' he said with great

concern. 'It is so dangerous.' And he begged us not to do it again.

He was concerned to know whether everything was to our satisfaction at Dekyi Lingka. Were we happy there? Were we being properly looked after? In fact his whole concern throughout the entire interview was for our welfare. We were the ones that mattered to him; he did not seem to think about himself at all. For the first time in my life I seemed to have had the good fortune to meet a genuinely selfless person. He was also practical. One might have anticipated that a great spiritual leader would be too preoccupied with exalted matters to be concerned about the petty details of ordinary life, but this was clearly not the case with His Holiness.

I am not a Buddhist—I have been a Christian all my life—yet there was an atmosphere in that little chamber. Something emanated from His Holiness. He was clearly a deeply spiritual man, and yet, as I have said, spiritual in a very down-to-earth sort of way. This was again borne out about three-quarters of the way through the interview, when he turned to Ringang and directed a question to me through him.

'You must be Captain Marshall's sister?'

'Yes, I am,' I replied.

I was really very surprised. One would not have thought that so great a man would have known the name of a military officer in charge of the Escort at Gyantse who had at one time given gunnery training to Yutok Se, Jigme Taring and members of the royal bodyguard. My brother Bill Marshall had indeed been that officer.

After about half an hour Derrick took the initiative in terminating the audience by getting up, bowing and leaving the room. Tennant and I followed, and finally Rai Bahadur Norbhu, who made his exit backwards.

'That was quite remarkable!' I said to Derrick as we remounted our ponies. I felt strangely uplifted, every perception clear as a bell, the world around me radiant.

After leaving His Holiness we went to call on the Lönchen or Prime Minister, Yapshi Kung, who had an office in the grounds of the Norbhu Lingka that we reached by a round-about route. I was surprised to find him so young—only about thirty. He seemed very friendly but Derrick did not get a very favourable impression, finding him rather empty and conceited.

The Lönchen returned our visit after we had returned to Dekyi Lingka and stayed to lunch. Later three of the Shapés called. They were ministers of the four-man Kashag or Cabinet, which was usually composed of an equal number of laymen and monastics. The head Shapé was a monk, the Kalön Lama, but the most influential was a layman, Trimön Shapé, who had been to India as assistant to the Tibetan plenipotentiary at the Simla Conference of 1914. He had recently lost his wife and as a result had also lost all interest in life. We were told that his advice was usually requested and respected by his colleagues in the Kashag. If, on the other hand, there was no consensus of opinion in the Kashag on any particular matter, then usually that of the Kalön Lama prevailed.

After tea, official business being done with for the moment, we were able to go and do some sightseeing around Lhasa. Our Tibetan guides and their syces rode ahead with our two chaprassys, then came Derrick and myself; Samdup and the clerks; and finally more messengers and grooms bringing up the rear. Out of the gates of Dekyi Lingka we rode, past the numerous beggars that seemed to have taken up permanent residence there since our arrival, and onto the broad motor road which took us past the Medical College (Chakpori), perched on its rocky eminence, and eventually to the three great *chörtens* which served as the western gateway to Lhasa. Immediately beyond them the Potala burst dramatically into view, its giant cambered walls bright with whitewash, soaring above us to a height of nearly 500 feet. Altogether it was a marvellously proportioned building, with stone staircases zigzagging across its rambling façade. When official ceremonies required it the Dalai Lama lived in a high central section, painted a deep red, where a gigantic yak-hair curtain hung. At other times he preferred the Norbhu Lingka with its pleasant gardens.

We rode past a *döring*—a stone column covered with Tibetan inscriptions—and near by came across two criminals wearing heavy wooden boards around their necks. The names of the offences they had committeed were written there for all the world to see. Apart from this, however, the two men seemed to be allowed to go about quite freely and get what livelihood they could for themselves by begging. It must have been difficult for them to sleep because the cumbersome boards would make it virtually impossible to lie down properly.

Further along we came to the Yutok Sampa, a covered bridge with a roof of the most exquisite turquoise tiles. It was frequented by many beggars and some of the mangiest dogs I had ever seen. We passed quickly on our way and came upon the gateway to the bazaar. Inside all was bustle with various kinds of vegetables, brightly coloured silks, burnished new brass and copper-ware, and many other curious and incongruous things being offered for sale. Here were people of every type: herders from the northern plains with long hair and greasy sheepskin clothing, merchants from Nepal, India and China, and even one or two Mongols from far to the north. They had seen European men before, but I was only the fourth European woman to come to Lhasa and they apparently thought me a tremendous joke. Crowding round, staring, pointing, poking each other and laughing, they would certainly have tried to touch me had our chaprassys not been there to keep them at bay! I found the situation quite amusing. It was about the only time during our stay in Lhasa when Derrick was virtually ignored!

The town of Lhasa itself, which is situated well away from the Potala and the Norbhu Lingka, was rather smaller than I had expected, but the houses were solidly built of stone and the main roads were wide and clean. Unfortunately, the same could not be said for the side streets. There was sewage and refuse everywhere, which was offensive both to the eyes and to the nose!

About 20,000 people lived there but the population swelled enormously when thousands of monks came pouring in for the annual Mönlam festival which follows the New Year. They would take over the running of the place for the duration and, as some of them were quite rowdy, many of the politically influential lay folk for whom the monks had little liking would leave temporarily until the excitement died down.

As we made our way round to the old parade-ground, we passed women washing clothes in a stream. Lots of high-spirited children were also running in and out of the water with much splashing and noise. I was astonished to see what fair skins the young girls had.

MUCH OF OUR TIME IN LHASA was taken up with social engagements, for it was important that we get to know people, and it was hoped that we British might thereby be able to exert a positive influence in Tibet. Some of the dinner parties we attended went on for hours with numerous exotic Chinese dishes, like shark's fin soup, sea slugs and various kinds of chicken and duck. We were therefore grateful for the occasional day off when we could relax with our mail and the newspapers that had followed us up from India. A particular social asset was the cinema. As in Bhutan, Charlie Chaplin was the great favourite; we had one of his films called *The Adventurer*, in which he played an escaped convict. The Tibetans renamed this film 'Kuma' (The Thief) and everyone wanted to see it, including His Holiness, who laughed heartily throughout the performance. The Tibetans all had a marvellous sense of humour. We were also able to show them films we had recently shot in Bhutan, these having been forwarded to us from Calcutta where they had been sent to be developed.

Generosity was a universal virtue among our Tibetan

friends and all our callers brought us presents, either on their first visit or when they came to say goodbye. Usually we received katas, a whole sheep (ready skinned), rice, grain and eggs. The eggs, alas, seemed to be rather more for the giving than for the eating, and many of them must have served as presents on quite a number of occasions for they almost invariably turned out to be rotten when broken! Derrick personally presented our gifts to the Dalai Lama, the Lönchen and the Shapés; the remainder were sent round to their recipients by messenger.

Our social encounters passed off very pleasantly as the Tibetans are by nature warm, sociable and scrupulous in their observance of good manners. We encountered one unfortunate exception to this general rule, however, during another visit we paid to the Lönchen on our fourth day. We had gone to his private house near the parade-ground. The visit began well enough. His pleasant young wife spoke a little English and we attempted to teach her some more. She had some difficulty with pronunciation, however, which we all found very funny. I also admired her hair, which was done in the Lhasa style, and her jewellery which included a pair of long turquoise earrings, a charm box and necklaces of lovely carved jade and pearls mixed with glass beads.

During the course of this meeting, we were treated to a fine Tibetan lunch of many dishes. However, both Derrick and I were horrified at our host's lack of manners. He helped himself first to every course, which was considered very bad manners in Tibet. He also placed himself on a much higher level than us, something Derrick felt was a deliberate snub to the British Government. A few Tibetan families had chairs and other pieces of Western furniture in their homes, but mostly we sat upon bodens and this had been the case at the Lönchen's. As I was to observe later, several bodens could be placed one on top of another to make a high seat for an important person, or a lower seat could be provided for someone less important.

Later Derrick sent Rai Bahadur Norbhu to see the Lönchen

privately to explain his feelings on the matter and when we visited him on other occasions Derrick was always seated at exactly the same height as his host. This was, however, the only time during our seven weeks in Lhasa when we encountered discourtesy.

Naturally we found it in many ways easiest to mix with those Tibetans who knew English and something of British ways. Among them could be counted the boys who had been to Rugby School. One of them, Gongkar, had died in the interim. It was said that he had fallen in love with an English girl and pined away because the Tibetan Government had refused to allow him to marry her; also that he had been deeply frustrated in his efforts to introduce new and more efficient military methods in eastern Tibet, where he had received a posting. An unhappy man, he had eventually succumbed to pneumonia. The remaining three boys were still very much alive, however, though Kyipup was also a rather sad individual and, like Gongkar, had never really settled down in Tibet after his return. He worked as a clerk in the new electrical installation at Trapchi. Mondö, the monk, on the other hand was in charge of the government storehouses in the Potala and elsewhere. Of all the Rugby boys, Ringang, the youngest, seemed to have made out the best. He acted as interpreter for the Dalai Lama, who put a great deal of trust in him; he was also a director of the new electrical works. Ringang and his two wives entertained us in their home and showed us their fine collection of family thangkas.

We also met boys who had been educated by Frank Ludlow at the short-lived English-type school set up in Gyantse in 1923. One of them, Sonam Dela Rabden, who was about twenty-five and rather shy, had lately been commissioned in the army but, quickly growing disenchanted with military life, had bought himself out after only fifteen days. He had had to have his long locks shorn but rather liked his new haircut and promised us that he intended to keep it when he got back to his family estate near Shigatse.

Besides the Ringangs, we saw much of Jigme and Mary-la

Taring, who were a most handsome couple. Mary-la was one of the seven daughters of the first Tsarong Shapé, who was a victim of the political upheavals following the expulsion of the Chinese from Lhasa in 1912. Accused of having been a collaborator, he was arrested in the Kashag office in the Potala, brutally hurled down the long stairway to the magistrates' building below and there done to death. Later his son was also killed. Following the triumphant restoration of the Dalai Lama in 1913, the Tsarong name and properties were bestowed upon Chensal Namgang, the son of a humble arrow-smith who had won His Holiness's favour for heroically assisting him in his escape from Lhasa in 1910 by holding off a pursuing Chinese force at the Tsangpo ferry.

Mary-la had been sent as a child to Darjeeling to receive an English education. There she had also learnt to bob her hair and to wear Western clothing, as well as picking up many other modern European ways. She had acquired the name Mary at school, though her real name was Rinchen Dolma. Her many accomplishments, including her command of English, made her immensely useful to the new Tsarong, a progressively minded man who conducted various business dealings with British India and other foreign countries. Having already married two of her older sisters, eventually he proposed marriage to Mary, making it clear that, as a man many years her senior, he would be prepared to stand aside gracefully should a more suitable husband ever present himself to her.

Jigme Taring, on the other hand, was the scion of the princely Tibetan family related to the Sikkimese royal house and at one time had been the heir-apparent to the throne of Sikkim. He too had received a good English education at St. Paul's School in Darjeeling and later entered the Tibetan Government service. At the time of our first visit to Lhasa he was second-in-command of the new army regiment at Trapchi, holding a rank equivalent to our Lieutenant-Colonel.

Jigme and Mary-la, having in common the benefits of an

English education, had known each other slightly since their Darjeeling days but, though a liking had developed, this had not blossomed into anything romantic. However, Tsarong recognized that what they had in common would serve as a useful foundation for an alliance, so he suggested that they marry. This they did, and a highly successful marriage it was.

Jigme and Mary-la came to visit us a great deal at Dekyi Lingka and I grew very fond of them, a relationship that I am pleased to say has survived the intervening half century. Derrick and I also visited them in the delightful little Alice in Wonderland house that had been built for them in the grounds of Tsarong House. We were often entertained at Tsarong House itself, which put me in mind of an English country house with its drive bordered with hollyhocks.

Tsarong Dzasa, who Derrick told me was something of an Anglophile, greeted us at the head of the steps to the house. His senior wife, Pema Dolkar, his son, Dundul, and Mary-la were also there to greet us. Tsarong was a short man, dressed in a strange mixture of western and Tibetan dress. His eyes, his whole bearing, clearly showed unusual energy, will, courage and intelligence.

Tsarong House had many Western-style appointments. There was a brass bedstead in the master bedroom; and the main staircase was fairly substantial, in contrast to the rickety ladder that served in most Tibetan households. The bathroom, too, did not have the usual hole in the floor but had Western fittings; and there was a large table and real chairs in the dining-room. The house was not only large but unusually clean and airy for a Tibetan house, many of which were rather dark. Tsarong House even had glass in the windows. Another surprise was when I was offered 'real' tea and biscuits. Then I felt truly at home.

The gardens at Tsarong House were also impressive. The soil and climate of Lhasa are excellent, and not only can up to three crops a year be obtained but the size of everything is quite remarkable. There were marvellous cauliflowers, cab-bages, onions, carrots, lettuces, radishes and turnips that would easily have won first prizes at any English country show.

One of Tsarong's hobbies—and a very unusual one in Lhasa at that time—was photography, and he had a collection of cameras. On one occasion when we were at his house, while the men talked in the vast sitting-room, the ladies took me to his office to show me his photograph albums. Later we played an original version of Snakes and Ladders that he had devised himself. There were entertainments too, usually Tibetan music and dancing.

Of the other Tibetans whom we got to know, Derrick and I were most impressed by Kunphel-la. His Holiness was very fond of him and showered him with wealth and favours. As a consequence Kunphel-la had been able to acquire for himself a fine house in Lhasa and to fill it with many rare and beautiful objects. He also had the use of His Holiness's second Baby Austin car, TIBET No. 2, which was painted blue.

Aware of the high favour in which he stood, Kunphel-la could be arrogant. His manners were faultless, however, and whenever we visited him he was invariably an impeccable and delightful host. He was also very handsome, and I said to Derrick that it was a very good thing that he was a monk or else the ladies of Lhasa would be breaking their hearts over him. Despite his religious vocation, Kunphel-la had a good grasp of worldly matters and had accomplished quite remarkable things out at Trapchi, where he was chief director of the new installations. He spent much time with Derrick discussing business matters, including the supply of munitions.

As we both got to know and like Kunphel-la more and more, the fact that he had many powerful enemies saddened us. Being a progressive force in the country—and a very effective one—he had unavoidably attracted the enmity of many of the conservatives, notably the malevolent Lungshar Tsepön.

Lungshar had been Commander-in-Chief of the Army from April 1929 until early in 1933 and for a few years he had himself ridden high in the favour of the Dalai Lama; but for at least a year prior to our visit his power had been waning. By confiscating the estates of many of the gentry when he had been in power, he had made himself most unpopular with them. Changlochen Kusho, who was one of our guides, particularly disliked him. Lungshar, moreover, had a reputation for being anti-British. While he was in England with the boys who were sent to Rugby, for instance, our agents had to keep a close watch upon him for he was up to all kinds of underhand tricks, making secret overtures not only to the Chinese but to the Russians as well. He had an incurable propensity for political intrigue, as later came out very forcibly, and was altogether a proud, arrogant and highly ruthless man.

What little we saw of Lungshar during the visit left no adverse impressions, however. He was friendly to Derrick as he had been to Derrick's predecessor. Unable to call on us when we first arrived in Lhasa, because, so he said, his health was not good, he sent us presents instead. Later we went to call on him and his wife in their house in Lhalu just outside Lhasa. I believe the gardens at Lhalu had been created by the Sixth Dalai Lama who, having grown tired of living in the dour Potala, went up onto the roof one day and fired three arrows in the hope that one would land in a place suitable for making a pleasant garden and where the water would also be good. One arrow struck ground too near, the second went too far, but the third landed in Lhalu, which by chance had an excellent spring. Some of the best water we had in Lhasa came from this spring.

7   Life in the Holy City

LHASA SEEMED PERVADED by a spirit of happy contentment which seemed to me to be the product of the Tibetans' Buddhist faith. I saw evidence of spiritual devotion every-where − and not only in the great monasteries and temples where one would have expected to encounter it. Every ordinary home had its shrine, perhaps even a shrine-room, while as often as not prayer-flags crowned the roof. Even in the street people turned their prayer-wheels or told their rosaries, or could be seen prostrating before some sacred shrine. There were berobed monks and nuns and of course pilgrims who had come to the holy city across the length and breadth of Central Asia. One saw too, on occasion, those particularly ardent pilgrims who had come to Lhasa and were now touring its circumambulation routes by means of pros-tration, measuring their full length upon the ground the whole way. They usually wore tattered leather protective coverings.

The pageantry and colour of Tibetan life impressed me greatly. An almost universal love of dressing-up as well as of ritual and ceremony was always in evidence, but particularly so on the festive occasions, which are liberally scattered throughout the calendar. The great festivals of the year were those taking place around the Tibetan New Year in February or March.

At the end of the old year there is a festival called Gutor, during which, in both homes and temples, rituals are enacted that are designed to cast out the negative accumulations of the previous twelve months and to wind up all unfinished business. Monks wearing grotesque masks perform elaborate dances symbolic of the eternal war between good and evil, while in homes people go through every room with lighted torches, shouting and letting off fire crackers and guns to scare off any evil spirits that may be lingering in dark corners. These necessary preliminaries having been accomplished, all is ready for the new year to get off to a good start. The New Year Festival itself, Losar, lasts for about a week. On the first day people get up early, wash, put on special clothes, place offerings on their household shrines and of course wish each other *'Tashi delek'*. Then children come round singing songs and wishing everyone long life. And so Losar goes on, with a great deal of merrymaking, feasting, dancing and present giving. Mönlam Chenmo, the Great Prayer Festival, immediately follows and lasts for about twenty-one days. Before 1959, Lhasa used to be taken over by the monks for the duration of this festival. There were monk magistrates and policemen in place of the usual ones. It was also the time when examinations were held in the great monasteries and degrees awarded to the most scholarly monks, or *geshes* as they were called. The highlight of Mönlam Chenmo was the Butter Festival, when the monks vied with one another to produce elaborate bas-reliefs in coloured butter on frames of wood and leather. Exotic ritual dances were also performed.

Derrick and I were in Lhasa at the right time to witness a performance of the opera-spectacle Ache Lhamo held at the Norbhu Lingka during three days. The Dalai Lama invited us to the second and third days, which were regarded as the most important.

A marvellously festive atmosphere greeted us when we awoke for we could hear the bugles playing as the troops were marched down to the Norbhu Lingka. For this formal affair, Derrick put on full dress uniform and Captain Tennant service dress. We arrived at the Norbhu Lingka at eleven o'clock, and were accommodated in a tent at the entrance to a great crazy-paved courtyard immediately opposite the tent of the Lönchen. The Dalai Lama watched unseen by the rest of the audience from a splendid lattice-fronted pavilion raised about ten feet above the ground. On either side and at various levels according to rank were pitched the tents of other monastic and lay officials, as well as those of the Nepalese and Bhutanese agents. There was a tent for the ladies too. Numerous less-exalted officials, monks and soldiers were also watching, all again seated hierarchically on bodens adjusted to the appropriate height. I myself was slightly apprehensive lest we too would have to spend the whole day sitting on bodens, but on entering our tent I was pleased to find that comfortable camp chairs had been provided for us.

A chorus of two men in beautiful brocade chubas, one wearing a red mask, was explaining the play, which was being performed by a troupe of colourfully attired actors down at the other end of the courtyard. Scenes of high drama or tragedy were interspersed with comic interludes. Stories from Tibetan history were enacted: the exploits of great kings and lamas, and the interventions of gods and spirits. There was much mime and whirling dance, most of it brilliantly done to the occasional accompaniment of cymbal and drum. The actors, all male, belonged to a travelling troupe that went all over Tibet. Once a year they came to Lhasa to offer His Holiness a free show as a kind of tax.

While in theory there was everything here to stimulate one's interest, the drama turned out to be rather tedious and I could soon feel Derrick growing restive in his tight uniform beside me. Thankfully, Indian tea was served us at regular intervals. Derrick found that the worst thing was that he couldn't smoke. Official opinion in Lhasa regarded tobacco as a pernicious drug and smoking was forbidden in public.

Another welcome relief came at lunchtime when we were able to leave the performance to eat an excellent meal provided for us by the Tibetan Government. The actors continued throughout our absence and were still going strong when we returned for the afternoon session. From time to time His

Holiness kindly sent to ask if we were enjoying ourselves. Of course we were most tactful in our replies.

My straying attention was now drawn to the antics of the giant monk guards, who were armed with fearsome leather thong whips. The mere sight of these whips was enough to keep the crowd in order, but the guards were quite ready to use them, even on minor officials, if they deemed it necessary. A guard also stood in front of the Dalai Lama's pavilion and was changed every half hour. I was quite concerned to see that one soldier was obviously asleep for most of his turn of duty.

At about half past four, large quantities of *ata* (whole wheat) bread, together with dried apricots and white sweets, were distributed. As all this food had been prepared in the Dalai Lama's kitchens, it was considered very holy. Instead of eating it, everybody wrapped their portion in a white cloth and took it away with them. When at about five o'clock the troops all lined up and began to play our National Anthem I thought this might be for us. I was mistaken, however: it was for His Holiness, who had adopted the piece for his own use. Thankfully, we were able to slip away shortly afterwards, though the play was still in full spate.

The drama continued next day. Towards the end a strong-man appeared and lay down on some bodens. Six men placed a huge stone on his stomach. Next a man tapped this six times with another stone before two men came up and, wielding large hammers, smashed the huge stone into small pieces. The strong-man then got up from his ordeal apparently un-scathed.

The grand finale consisted of rewards for the actors. They lined up and barley flour (*tsampa*), grain, chang and money in bags were brought out for them. The katas and small pieces of cloth that had been blessed were wrapped round their necks by the giant guards and other officials. After that, each actor stepped forward in turn, took a handful of flour and went to form a line facing the Dalai Lama's pavilion and flung the flour high into the air, at the same time exclaiming, *'Lhagyelo!'* ('Victory to the gods!'). A great white cloud billowed out above them as they prostrated themselves three times before his Holiness.

DERRICK OF COURSE HAD VARIOUS MEETINGS during our stay in Lhasa, at which government business was discussed. He had a few private meetings with His Holiness, at which Rai Bahadur Norbhu accompanied him. On the 21 September, for instance, he went to the Norbhu Lingka and stayed from about half past nine until noon, talking and taking photographs both in the reception room and in the garden.

His Holiness had apparently expressed his appreciation of the Government of India's friendly attitude over such matters as the levy of customs duties on his own private imports and the arrangements for payment for the latest consignment of munitions. The subject of the exiled Panchen Lama had also come up. Recently he had sent representatives to Lhasa to hold discussions about his return, and Derrick met them in Kalimpong in April on their way up. The demands they had put had not pleased His Holiness – in particular that the Panchen Lama should have all troops recruited in Tsang province under his control. Also His Holiness objected to some of the exiled Lama's 'intimate friends', believing them to be trouble-makers. Derrick for his part urged the Dalai Lama to be generous, bearing in mind the good treatment that the Panchen Lama was currently receiving in China. He 'professed to agree', but Derrick had the strong feeling that really he was not at all in favour of securing a return. The Tibetan people, on the other hand, were universally in favour of seeing the Panchen Lama restored to Tashilhunpo. Derrick's own view was that the British should encourage a return and certainly not discourage it. He was a little concerned, however, that in their eagerness to secure a return the Tibetan Government might forget or neglect to impose proper conditions for it, in which case the Panchen Lama might bring a Chinese escort back with him. His Holiness was very frank and clear with Derrick about his attitude to the Chinese: he did not want a Chinese official ever to visit Lhasa as all the Chinese wanted to do was to pave the way for a renewal of Chinese domination.

Derrick was pleased with this meeting, feeling that he had won the Dalai Lama's trust. He was concerned, however, by the state of His Holiness's health. I was worried that Derrick had taken his dog along with him to this meeting, for I was afraid His Holiness might want to keep Bruce. However, he fortunately thought him too big and wanted something smaller to tuck up beside him as a hot water bottle!

Derrick also visited the *Kashag* (Cabinet) in their offices in the Jokhang. These were rather formal affairs. The Shapés were always ceremonially dressed on these occasions in their yellow silk robes of office, with their hair done up in topknots. Katas were exchanged and then there was tea and general conversation before any business was broached.

Besides those with His Holiness and the Kashag, Derrick also had less formal business meetings with the Lönchen, the Shapés, Kunphel-la and other high officials. He was invariably most sensitive and tactful, aiming always to get to know the people involved as well as possible and to get on friendly terms with them. Thus relationships of mutual trust and respect could be set up, making agreement easier to arrive at than if a less harmonious atmosphere prevailed. It should always be remembered too that Derrick could only rely upon persuasion in order to achieve the aims of the British Government vis-à-vis Tibet; he had no more powerful cards up his sleeve. He also had to be scrupulously aware of local protocol and do nothing that might arouse offence or suspicion. In a way, then, his work was a delicate balancing act. The fact that he achieved such success in it attests to how skilful a diplomat he was.

MEANWHILE, I WAS OTHERWISE EMPLOYED. During that first visit to Lhasa I managed to organize two social events that were entirely new departures for the Tibetan capital: a children's party and a ladies' party.

We held our children's party on 2 September. Our young guests were due to arrive at half past two but the first of them began to show up at eleven and Norbhu had to keep them at bay for three hours while we frantically got on with the preparations, in which we were kindly assisted by Jigme and Mary-la Taring, Dingcha and several other Tibetan friends. Over forty children came and had great fun and games. We laid on a treasure hunt for them, a potato race, musical bumps, an egg-and-spoon race (with real eggs, which, thankfully, they mostly managed not to break!), a sack-race and a thread-and-needle race. Then there was a huge tea complete with fruit jelly, which they had never seen before and which caused a great deal of merriment! Afterwards we took them inside for a cinema show, putting on Fritz the Cat and Charlie Chaplin, which caused more hilarity. They were all presented with prizes and eventually they left—with enormous reluctance!—around half past five, each child carrying away a little package of the resourceful Pinjo's excellent toffee. It all went off happily and I was told on good authority that it was certain to be the talk of Lhasa for months to come as nothing of the kind had ever happened there before.

There is an interesting postscript that I should mention here. In 1974, I was invited to attend the coronation of the fourth king of Bhutan, Jigme Singhe Wangchuk, whom I had first met when he was a boy at school in England. Afterwards, I took the opportunity of going on from Bhutan to Sikkim to renew my acquaintance with some of my old friends there. One day while walking in the palace grounds in Gangtok a Tibetan monk approached me, apparently very keen that I should see around the royal temple, of which he was clearly the guardian. After I had obliged him and made a visit, he began to try and tell me something but, in the absence of a common language, I could not understand him at all. Finally we located someone who could interpret for us and then to my amazement and pleasure I found out that as a young boy this monk had been a guest at the children's party held in Lhasa in 1933 and that he still warmly remembered the occasion.

The ladies' party was held on 19 September and was attended by twenty-three Lhasa ladies and about a dozen children who for some reason or other had been unable to come to the children's party. The ladies looked most picturesque in their colourful clothes and exquisite jewellery. Most of them wore their hair in the Lhasa style, built up into two pinnacles on a triangular frame decorated with seed pearls and corals. One or two, however, sported the Gyantse style, which is more elaborate, incorporating a semi-circular hoop with various parts, again all decorated with pearls and corals. While it looked most regal, one could not help feeling that it must also be most uncomfortable to wear!

We began with a cinema show and then Pinjo laid on a sumptuous tea. Lhasa ladies used only to mix in very restricted circles and so this occasion was a great novelty; it allowed them to meet and talk with others whom they would never in the normal course of things have an opportunity to meet. They all appeared to enjoy themselves immensely and many came to call on me later.

WE DID MANAGE TO MAKE a few spaces in our busy diplomatic and social schedule to see the more significant places of interest in and around Lhasa. In Western countries this kind of sightseeing usually involves visits to museums and to carefully preserved historical remains, but in Lhasa the antiquities were still very much in use and had been so for centuries. This, linked to the fact that there was so little evidence of modern development, was a constant reminder that we were in a society which was in many ways still in the Middle Ages, though this is not to say that it was decadent. It was a rich culture, with a deep underlying sense of continuity and spirituality.

On 27 August, we set off on a long-awaited visit to the Potala. The name '*Potala*' is said to derive from that of an island off the southernmost tip of India reputed to be the abode of Avalokiteshvara, the Bodhisattva of Compassion, who is known in Tibet as Chenrezig and of whom the Dalai Lama is an emanation. There has been a building on the rocky outcrop here (once known as the Red Hill) since the time of King Trisong Detsen (741–798), during whose enlightened reign Buddhism was first established in Tibet. The palace he built was, however, swept away by war and the present structure was begun by the Great Fifth Dalai Lama in the seventeenth century; it was completed soon after his death. No one really knows how much of the pre-existing building was incorporated into it.

I found the Potala an amazingly interesting place. We were conducted through a labyrinth of corridors into numerous shrine-rooms and other rooms which, although small and rather dark, contained ancient images, paintings and other objects. We were also shown a couple of fairly large assembly halls, in one of which we were told Colonel Younghusband and his Tibetan opposite number had signed the Treaty of 1904. The climax of our visit were the great gilded and bejewelled chörtens right up in the roof in which were deposited the remains of departed Dalai Lamas. By far the most lavish was that of the Great Fifth, above which was an image containing a collection of every possible type of precious stone.

Thankfully we were not shown the dungeons of the Potala, in which prisoners were said to languish, nor did we see the strong-rooms in which the fabulous treasure of the Dalai Lamas was stored. We did, however, go out onto the flat roofs where, as the view was magnificent, we lingered for some time taking photographs. The city of Lhasa lay spread out on the flat valley floor below us, with its distant encircling wall of tangled mountains.

Later that same day we proceeded to Ramoche monastery, close to the Lingkor, the circumambulation route that runs right round the holy city. At Ramoche the main temple of Gyu-tö, one of the two Tantric colleges in Lhasa, we found hundreds of monks engaged in a religious ceremony. Each held a *dorje* in one hand and a bell to be rung at appropriate times in the other. Their chanting set up a powerful vibration that I found thrilling. We were also shown a couple of shrine-rooms, in one of which the religious images had been recently regilded and shone brightly. One saw so much gold in the religious buildings of the old Tibet.

We also visited the Jokhang, the Central Cathedral, that day. It dates back to the reign of the great seventh-century king Songtsen Gampo, and was built to house an image of the Buddha brought to Tibet by the king's Nepalese wife. The famous image brought by the king's Chinese wife, the Jowo Rinpoché, was also installed there around AD 725. Over the succeeding centuries the basic structure had been added to and was now a vast aggregation of shrine-rooms. These contained a great deal of fine carving and many precious paintings and images, but the butter lamps that provided illumination had also over the centuries covered everything with a patina of grease and grime.

My attention in the Jokhang was engaged by the hundreds of mice that infested the place. They were running about all over the sacred images and were responsible for a most unpleasant odour! Some were so tame that they even allowed Derrick to stroke them and a few had the impertinence to sit up on their hind legs and drink from the sacred water bowls! The application of the Buddhists' respect for life was responsible for their unchecked numbers and tameness.

Near the entrance of the Jokhang there was a relic of the time some two hundred years before when Catholic missionaries had been active in Lhasa. This was an old bell bearing the Latin inscription *Te Deum Laudamus*. The Tibetans traditionally had none of that suspicion of other faiths that blights so many religions, and are very tolerant. The Catholics in Lhasa were not tolerant, however, and stirred up a fair amount of strife by their attempts to turn the Tibetans against their own religion. It was this rather than any basic prejudice against Christianity which eventually led to their expulsion and to the subsequent Tibetan refusal to allow foreign missionaries on their soil.

From the Jokhang we went on to the Lukhang or House of Snakes. Near the entrance we encountered the two elephants that the Maharaja of Nepal had sent as a present to the Dalai Lama. We were paddled across a small lake in a wooden boat with a horse-head prow to a tiny island where the House of Snakes was situated. I approached with a certain amount of misgiving, but I need not have worried. There were no real snakes there, only sculptured ones: every image in fact had snakes entwined behind its head.

LHASA HAS THREE GREAT MONASTIC UNIVERSITIES in its vicinity: Drepung, Sera and Ganden. We were able to visit the first two in 1933.

We found Drepung to be a vast complex of whitewashed stone buildings, some of which had gilded roofs. It was situated on the lower slopes of a hillside about three miles outside Lhasa and dates from the fifteenth century. We saw few of its vast population of some 7,700 monks, for as we proceeded on our sightseeing tour a man went ahead of us, shouting to warn them to stay in their rooms. It was feared that otherwise they might be a nuisance to us.

There are four colleges at Drepung, each headed by its own abbot; we visited them all and were given sweetened milk and rice in each. I was impressed by the marvellous images, paintings and other religious objects that we saw everywhere, many of them very old and some of great size. Of great size too were the copper cauldrons we saw in the kitchens, which were used for brewing the monks' tea. After our monk-guide had kindly given us lunch, we were able to purchase some souvenirs of our visit to Drepung. We bought a pair of the heavy iron maces carried by the *shengos* (the monastic proctors) and an earthenware teapot with brass decoration.

Our visit to Sera took place about four days later. Sera was also about five miles from Lhasa, beyond Trapchi, and was in many ways similar to Drepung though on a smaller scale. It housed about 5,500 monks. No attempt was made to keep them to their rooms—and I am pleased to say that they caused us no nuisance.

An interesting sight at Sera was a monastic debate in progress. Tibetan monks, particularly those of the Gelug order, spend much time being trained in the intricacies of Buddhist philosophy and this involves sharpening their powers of reasoning, argument and scriptural reference. From time to time they practise or demonstrate these powers, along with a great deal of formalized rhetorical posturing and gesticulation. The monastic debaters we saw in action seemed to be demolishing their opponents' arguments physically as well as intellectually!

On one of our visits a monk cast horoscopes for us. He did this by shaking a wooden box until a stick fell out; then he scrutinized the number on the stick and looked up the corresponding entry in a thick book. At my suggestion Derrick took out his fountain pen and began to scribble notes about our characters: '... straight-forwardness, one who takes a lively interest in life, clearness of ideas, average type, conscientiousness, painstaking nature, very selfish and somewhat reticent, very suspicious, secretiveness, excellent imagination and keen vision, particular adaptability to work and tasks requiring precision and exactness, energy, ambition, ardour, modesty, high sense of honour coupled with con- siderable dignity...' Unfortunately, in his haste Derrick did not have time to record to whom the various traits applied, so we had to try to work that out for ourselves afterwards. One thing I am perfectly clear about, however, is that the astrologer predicted to Rai Sahib Bo that all his patients would die!

Another visit I remember well was one we made to the grounds of the Norbhu Lingka. We were escorted round the beautifully kept gardens by Kunphel-la and Ringang. We followed flagged paths that wove through them and admired the profusion of blooms on every side. There were lupins, nasturtiums, sunflowers, hollyhocks, stocks and roses. There were also dogs of various breeds—dachshunds, dalmatians, pekinese and many ferocious Tibetan mastiffs—not to mention three monkeys and a bear.

In a small rest-house the Dalai Lama kept his collection of exquisite jade carvings and *cloisonné* brought back with him from his exile in China. There was also a lake in which a delightful little temple had been built. This was surrounded by stone balustrades and pots of flowers, and on the outside walls were painted panels. Here a scribe was seated cross-legged, so deeply engrossed in his work that his nose nearly touched the paper.

Outside one of the many small temples we found a tiger and a leopard—both stuffed—and a pair of brass lions. In the stables were real animals: about 150 horses and mules. Since the Dalai Lama had acquired his motor cars, however, they were only used once a year for the great ceremonial procession to the Potala.

Down a broad avenue of poplar trees we found Chense Lingka, meaning 'favourite garden', which consisted of another private palace and garden that Kunphel-la had recently designed and had built for His Holiness. Here more flowers bloomed and we saw the bower where His Holiness liked to sit in the afternoon. Behind the main palace was another small palace with a sun-room at the rear.

In our tour of this miniature wonderland of palaces, temples and gardens, we came at length to a path lined with trees—and from every tree hung a cage with a little bird in it. This delightful aviary-walk brought us past another summer house to the garages where His Holiness's cars were stored. The first car, acquired about two years before our visit, was a Baby Austin bearing the numberplate TIBET No. 1. Painted yellow and red, its interior was lined with Chinese brocade. Later a six-cylinder Dodge had been added which was brightly painted, had no number and seemed to have its hood permanently raised. Yellow silk trim had been put around the windows and the rear seat covered with yellow brocade.

Lastly, there was the blue Baby Austin, TIBET No. 2, which Kunphel-la was permitted to use. The cars had to be transported in pieces over the mountains and the petrol brought up in cans.

We walked back around the palace and looked into a large audience chamber, the centrepiece of which was a huge throne with a gold-washed table beside it. Here our tour was interrupted by a servant who had brought smoked glass from the Dalai Lama. An eclipse of the sun was anticipated and His Holiness in his infinite kindness wished us to be able to see it. Later we were given an excellent lunch on the verandah of the audience chamber and then, after we had seen over an old coach-house containing an assortment of dandies, buggies, sedan-chairs and carriages, we went to call on the Chikyap Khenpo, a pleasant old gentleman who was officially disciplinary head of all the monks in Tibet.

I have already emphasized the lack of modern development in Tibet, but there were a few significant exceptions to the general rule. The Dalai Lama's motor cars were one, and another was the establishment of a factory at Trapchi. Here, about three miles outside the holy city, Kunphel-la's forward-looking vision, energy and organizing genius were on full display. We paid two visits to the factory in 1933.

Our first visit took place at the invitation of Kunphel-la. He met us on arrival with a band and a guard of honour complete with flying colours. We visited the new workshops run on the electric power generated at Dote, some six miles away and the original site of the workshops. The electrical machinery had all been acquired by Ringang in England in 1924 and ran very quietly. Rather incongruously it had been installed in a room of many pillars gaily painted and decorated in the usual Tibetan style—not at all a typical factory interior. Silver coins were being cut, milled and stamped, bank-notes printed, rifle barrels bored, and shell and cartridge cases filled. The products were given their finishing touches by a row of workmen sitting on a verandah and using hand-tools. They sang merrily as they worked but the noise of their files set my teeth on edge.

Near by there was a large and well-built armoury in which several thousand rifles and a large quantity of ammunition were stored. Apparently there were plans afoot to build more rooms for the storage of machine-guns and other weapons. When we next visited Trapchi a few weeks later we were amazed to see that the projected new store-rooms had already been completed. Two hundred coolies, seventy carpenters and sixty masons had put them up in thirteen days flat. A little later, on the adjacent range, we saw some of the machine-guns in action. Accuracy was pretty good.

Kunphel-la surprised me by telling me that it was my brother who was responsible for the training of some of these men. I was touched once again that such a highly-placed person had noted that I was Bill Marshall's sister.

The regiment at Trapchi, which had been in existence for about six months, was commanded by Yutok Depön, a young man of about thirty who had received training both at Gyantse and at Quetta. His second-in-command was our friend Jigme Taring. The overall quality of the troops was, it seemed, a direct result of the special care taken in their recruitment.

TOWARDS THE END OF SEPTEMBER, as the mild summer days began to retreat before the onset of autumn, which itself carried intimations of the bitter Tibetan winter, the time for our departure from Lhasa drew near. We had seen so many wonderful things in the holy city; we had enjoyed a delight-ful 'home from home' at Dekyi Lingka; we had, I hope, done much useful work for our Government; but most of all we had everywhere received such kindness and made so many new friends that parting must inevitably be tinged with sadness.

Our departure was fixed for 4 October. As the day ap-proached, we were visited by large numbers of callers intent upon wishing us a cordial farewell.

We also had to take our leave of His Holiness. This really began on 29 September, when Derrick went by himself to have an audience in the morning. They discussed various matters and Derrick informed him of the date fixed for our departure. When Derrick returned to Dekyi Lingka for lunch, he was smiling broadly. His Holiness had invited us both back that evening. I was very thrilled by this invitation, for I had not seen His Holiness since our first official call.

When we arrived at Chense Lingka in the grounds of the Norbhu Lingka I was again wearing my French tweed suit. We were shown to His Holiness's room on the first floor, a long room of many pillars, decorated with beautiful paintings and carvings. The floor on the left hand side was brightly polished, while on the right, near the windows, lay a fine Chinese carpet. His Holiness sat on a throne at the far end. We exchanged katas and then sat drinking tea and eating peaches grown in his garden. Kunphel-la was also there, and both he and His Holiness were very friendly and informal.

Later we were shown films on His Holiness's projector which Captain Tennant, who had considerable technical expertise, had been able to put into good running order. The first film was of the Panchen Lama and had been taken in China and presented to His Holiness by the exiled Lama's representatives. Then we showed some of our own films, including footage shot in Lhasa which had been down to Calcutta for processing. For the viewing His Holiness got down from his throne and sat on chairs with us, with Kunphel-la the picture of filial devotion at his feet.

We rode over to the Norbhu Lingka to pay our official farewell to His Holiness on 2 October. Derrick looked splendid in his dress uniform. The event took place in the same room in which His Holiness had received us on our first official meeting. His Holiness received us and then blessed each of our servants. He finally gave us presents and asked Derrick to come and see him privately to say goodbye the next day.

We finally rode out of the grounds of Dekyi Lingka at ten o'clock on 4 October. It was a beautiful day to be taking to the road again but inevitably there was a great deal of formality to go through before we could begin our journey in earnest. As on arrival, there was a guard of honour and tea to be taken with the representatives of the Dalai Lama, the Lönchen and the Shapés. Then numerous other people waited to see us off at precisely the same places they had met us as we rode in. We parted from the last of the well-wishers near Drepung: then all that lay ahead of us was the stony road south.

*(Previous page) Lhochode
Lhakang, Sakya.*

Talung Monastery.

Sakya town.

*Hermit and Samdup touch
hands at Nyang-to Kyi-pup
Monastery.*

*(Opposite) The young
Rinpoché and his children visit
our camp at Sakya.*

The old Rinpoché in ceremonial dress.

The Nepalese Agent calls at Dekyi Lingka.

Tashilhunpo Monastery.

*The Dzasa Lama at
Tashilhunpo.*

(Opposite) Camp at Nagartse.

Towa Dzong. Bamboo for prayer flags brought from many miles away.

The Maharaja of Bhutan at Government House, Calcutta.

Derrick with the Maharajas of Bhutan and Sikkim.

(Following page) Maharaja of Bhutan and the Viceroy at Government House, Calcutta.

8   Death of a Dalai Lama

WE TRAVELLED HOMEWARDS by the direct route to Gangtok, the weather becoming progressively colder, reminding us that the bitterly cold Tibetan winter was now advancing fast. After six weeks on the road, on 15 November, we dropped from Penlong-la towards Gangtok and were met a mile and a half out by an official reception committee. Garlanded and toasted with *marwa* we drove back to the Residency in fine style in a small motor convoy, sent by His Highness.

Derrick and I began to readjust ourselves to the agreeable rhythms of life at the Residency. Then, a few short weeks after our return, news reached us of an event that was to plunge Tibet into crisis for a long time to come. While we attended a performance of dances at the Palace, Derrick received a telegram containing the stark message that the Dalai Lama had died on 17 December 1933.

I felt at once a wave of sadness, an initial response that was almost immediately replaced by deep anxiety. The Tibetans, I knew, were extremely suspicious of foreigners; might they then leap to the conclusion that our own recent visit to Lhasa had somehow contributed to His Holiness's passing?

'The repercussions are bound to be immense,' Derrick declared. 'It's hard to predict, of course; a lot will certainly depend on who is appointed Regent. According to precedent, it should be a monk. Tri Rinpoché, perhaps; he's often discharged the office in the past. The amount of power he actually wields will depend very much on how strong a personality he is and how well he can deal with the various

129

political factions. One thing is unfortunately certain, however,' he went on. 'Our friend Kunphel-la will be in an awkward position now. His great powers depended solely on His Holiness's favour.'

Telegrams of condolence were soon speeding along the wire to Lhasa from the Government of India, from the Viceroy and even from King George V in London.

Reports that we received from Lhasa in the days immediately following his Holiness's death suggested that the business of government was going on as usual and that all the high officials had retained their posts. Instead of undergoing political upheavals, Tibet entered a period of mourning, with prayers offered up for a speedy reincarnation of the Dalai Lama. The Tibetan Government did, however, warn the Chinese not to take advantage of the situation. They sent a firmly worded telegram to Nanking that stated, 'should any steps be taken as a result of the influence of persons who want to create trouble between the two countries, such action will not be tolerated, even if reduced to the last man in this country . . .'

Shortly afterwards, at the end of December, Derrick was surprised to receive a private letter from Lungshar Tsepön to the effect that the Chinese had written 'in a pressing manner' to the Lönchen, the Kashag and the National Assembly, telling them that they intended sending a representative to Lhasa at once. 'Therefore the British Government should pay attention to the matter,' Lungshar urged.

'Lungshar isn't usually noted for his pro-British, anti-Chinese sympathies,' Derrick remarked after reading this. 'I wonder what the wily devil is up to? And what's afoot with the Chinese?'

It was not long afterwards that we heard to our deep concern of the official Chinese Mission of Condolence under Huang Mu-sung.

Derrick received the first detailed news of developments in Lhasa from Jigme Taring. Jigme informed Derrick that there was some disagreement among the high officials as to what direction the political future of Tibet might take. Some of them were even apparently discussing the possibility of setting up some kind of republic. Nothing serious was likely to happen, however, until after the New Year festivities, which were due to start in February. As for Tsarong Dzasa himself, Jigme said that he was still away on his country estate.

'Jigme feels that this is for the best. High officials are notoriously vulnerable during times of political change in Tibet,' Derrick said. 'Look what happened to Mary-la's father [the first Tsarong, who had been killed]. On the other hand, it does mean that the most important friend of Britain is out of the political arena at this time, which could weaken our position.'

Other reports indicated that scapegoats were being sought for His Holiness's death. Blame was laid at the door of the Nechung Oracle, who was accused of having made a mistake over the Dalai Lama's medicine. He was degraded to the status of an ordinary monk. We heard too that the Dronyer Chempo, the Lord Chamberlain, had committed suicide by eating broken glass. Also, to our particular disquiet, fingers were pointed at Kunphel-la.

Reports reaching us via Captain Hailey in the early days of 1934 suggested that efforts were still being made to have Kunphel-la appointed joint Lönchen; also that the Kashag was having him closely watched.

Our worst anxieties were confirmed toward the middle of January. Reports reached us then that Kunphel-la had been arrested on the grounds of having been involved in a conspiracy to poison His Holiness. Brought before the Kashag, he was questioned as to whether it was true that he had petitioned His Holiness to make him joint Lönchen. He apparently admitted his guilt on this charge and was thereupon incarcerated in the Potala. His father and brother were also arrested; and his supporters, who included Yutok Depön and various army officers, became very worried that they too might be deprived of their liberty—or worse.

'The charges against him are clearly absurd!' Derrick exclaimed hotly when he heard the news. 'You saw how affectionate His Holiness and he were towards each other—like father and son.'

'Is there perhaps an ulterior motive?' I asked.

'Yes, indeed,' Derrick agreed. 'Hailey thinks the Shapés fear that Kunphel-la may be able to rally the military behind him. The three great monasteries seem to have agreed to the arrest.'

Kunphel-la's life now stood in dire peril, for he had many powerful enemies, notably the ruthless Lungshar, and there were calls for his execution—or at least that he should lose an arm or a leg. Fortunately, however, he had support among the ordinary monks. When it came to a final judgement, the abbots of the three great monasteries found that his fault, if any, was trifling. At the very worst he had merely conspired to conceal the Dalai Lama's death for a few days in order to gain some small advantage over his political rivals. His punishment was to be stripped of his very considerable wealth and exiled to the Chaknak monastery in Kongbo province, where he was appointed abbot. He eventually escaped through Bhutan to British India, where he settled in Kalimpong and earned his living managing a warehouse in which Tibetan wool was stored.

January also brought us the news that a Regent had been appointed. It was not to be the venerable Tri Rinpoché, as Derrick had speculated, but rather the young incarnate abbot of Reting monastery. We had not met him when we were in Lhasa but first reports did not give an entirely favourable impression. He was said to be very young—twenty-three years old, though at first Derrick was led to believe that he was only twelve!—and an inexperienced andministrator. It also seemed as though the mantle of the Regency had been forced upon him against his will. Though he was generally said to be charming and sympathetic to Britain, he hardly seemed the man of iron will for whom those critical times were crying out.

Following the departure of Kunphel-la, most of the news reports of political developments in Lhasa emphasized the growing power of Lungshar. He had apparently ingratiated himself with the great monasteries by liberally distributing largesse and had created a strong power base for himself in the National Assembly, which had now eclipsed the Kashag and was virtually running the country. Unfortunately, the elderly conservative Trimön Shapé, the leader of the Kashag, was simply no match for the formidable Lungshar, who hated him greatly. Tsarong Dzasa continued to stay at a safe distance on his country estate.

The first indication Derrick got that sinister plots were being fomented was on 26 April, when two of Lungshar's servants passed through Gangtok bearing letters addressed to him. The first was of no particular moment. It merely stated the opinion that it would be desirable for Derrick to visit Lhasa again that year in view of the disturbed situation and the threat of Chinese intrusion. The other letter, however, really caused Derrick to raise his eyebrows. It requested the British to supply Lungshar with thirty rifles, a Lewis gun and 31,000 rounds of ammunition. Although it would have been useful, in view of his great influence, if we could in some way have put Lungshar under an obligation to us, the request could not be entertained.

With this greed for power and insatiable propensity for intrigue, Lungshar had all the makings of a Central Asian Macbeth. Thus he drove himself to perform deeds that raised the next phase of political events in Lhasa to the level of high theatre. In the process, however, he became blind to all caution and overreached himself, thereby losing the support of the great monasteries.

The drama reached its climax on 10 May 1934. That day Lungshar and the National Assembly made a push for power, in the face of which Trimön Shapé fled Lhasa and sought refuge in Drepung monastery. Lungshar at once urged that action be taken against Trimön Shapé, but the Assembly refused to agree to this. Trimön was then able to turn the tables upon his adversary. Returning quickly to Lhasa, he arranged for Lungshar to be summoned before the Kashag at the Potala.

Lungshar appeared, swaggering characteristically and accompanied by a retinue of armed servants. At once he was seized and charged with having conspired to replace the legitimate government of Tibet with a Bolshevist regime.

Ruthless man that he was, Lungshar did not pass into custody meekly. He attempted to break free of his captors and reach his servants in order to gain possession of a pistol. There was a struggle, in the course of which one of the giant monks in the Kashag's service broke Lungshar's arm.

As a mark of degradation, Lungshar's official dress was at once torn off. He was divested of the gold charm box which was bound to his topknot of hair. His honorific boots were also removed—and when this was done unmistakable evidence of dark deeds was revealed: a small piece of paper fluttered to the floor. Lungshar immediately dived for it and managed to get it into his mouth and swallow it. When the second boot was examined, a similar piece of paper was found—and this bore the name of Trimön Shapé.

'It is a custom in Tibet that if anyone wishes to harm an enemy, spells are performed against him and his name is constantly trampled underfoot in this way,' Derrick explained to me. 'It's considered a certain way of bringing about either death or madness and for that reason is considered as foul a crime as murder.'

If Trimön Shapé's name was on one of the pieces of paper, no doubt the Regent, the Lönchen and the other Shapés were worried that their names might have been on the slip of paper that Lungshar had managed to swallow.

Attempts to secure Lungshar's release failed when the heads of the great monasteries became convinced of his guilt. He was tried, confessions having been extracted from his supporters that he had been conspiring to be made co-Regent and to have Trimön Shapé killed. The punishment clearly had to fit the crime, but I was shocked when I heard what it was.

On 20 May, Lungshar's eyes were put out and he was thrown into a dungeon.

Even with a broken arm, Lungshar apparently tried to escape from the room in which he had been confined. He managed to make a hole in the wall, though got no further than that.

Lungshar remained in confinement until 1938, when he was released. Hugh Richardson, who saw him at that time, reports that despite all the suffering and humiliation that he had endured, he was still a proud and arrogant man.

As for the earthly remains of the Dalai Lama, whose death led to these dramatic and tragic events, they were embalmed and a start was made upon creating a monumental chörten in which they could finally be laid to rest. The good people of Lhasa, with characteristic generosity and love of their spiritual and temporal ruler, began to liberally donate precious metals and stones as well as *objets d'art* for this tomb, which would eventually take its place alongside the tombs of the other Dalai Lamas in the Potala. His Holiness's apartments were kept scrupulously clean and his personal religious objects—such as his prayer-wheel, dorje and bell, stood ready on a small table in the Norbhu Lingka awaiting his eventual return.

Meanwhile, during his temporary absence, Tibetans felt highly vulnerable—and particularly so as the Panchen Lama was also absent from the land. They feared that forces hostile to a free Tibet might seize this moment to make a move. Indeed, the late Dalai Lama in a document known as his Shalchem or Final Testament had predicted as much:

> Very soon even in this land of the harmonious blend of religion and politics, such acts may occur forced from without or within. At that time, if we do not dare to protect our territory, our spiritual personalities, including the victorious father and son [the Dalai and Panchen Lamas] may be exterminated

without trace, the property and authority of our
Ladangs [office/residences of incarnate lamas] and
monks may be taken away. Moreover, our political
system ... will vanish without trace. The property
of all people, high and low, will be seized and the
people forced to become slaves. All living things
will have to endure endless days of suffering and
will be stricken with fear psychosis. Such a time will
come.*

Such warnings, delivered by one generally believed to have
been endowed with divine powers, were not to be taken
lightly.

*Translation from Tibetan by Bhuchung K. Tsering; printed in
Tibetan Bulletin, Dharamsala, Vol. XV, No. 4, pp 8–10

9 Life at the Residency

THE EVENTS IN Lhasa seemed a long way away from the tranquil life Derrick and I led at the Residency in Gangtok. Every morning we awoke to see the first sunlight reflected on the great snowy ridges of the Kanchenjunga Range. A tray of tea would be brought and we would linger, admiring the play of light, which changed from moment to moment as the sun climbed higher in the sky.

We had few modern conveniences at the Residency. The two bathrooms adjoining our bedroom had no hot water—if you wanted a bath you had to tell Karma, the water boy, and he would bring the hot water up from down below and fill the red tin bath. Karma's exclusive duties were to carry water; the sweepers, on the other hand, emptied the thunder-boxes (commodes), in the absence of modern sanitation.

In the morning we often went riding, then after breakfast Derrick would ensconce himself in his office. He would read *The Statesman*, which came up from Calcutta, and do the crossword. Then he would start work on his files.

Derrick's most urgent task on our return from the 1933 tour was to write a report, which was later typeset for circulation in official quarters. He was also at this period working on the Maharaja of Bhutan's behalf, trying to persuade the Government of India to increase its financial aid, a request the Maharaja had made during his official discussions with Derrick at Bumthang in July.

As for myself, it was very much left to me to decide how to spend my own time. I had a great deal to do, looking after my various duties. I cannot say that I was ever really pushed for time, but my days were always full. This was mainly because we had to spend so much time away: we were on tour in Tibet and Bhutan for four or five months each year and there were short tours of Sikkim to fit in as well. The result was that a great deal of activity had to be crammed into the limited time we were actually in residence in Gangtok.

I looked after the social side. As the only other place in Gangtok where Europeans could stay was the dak bungalow, we had to put many of them up at the Residency. Indeed, an endless stream of visitors seemed to flow through the house during our time there. As well as our friends, Government officials, Army people and even the occasional foreign ambassador were delighted to be able to find sanctuary with us from the heat of the plains.

All visitors to Sikkim in those days had to get official passes from the Deputy Commissioner in Darjeeling, so he could tell us who was coming and would often suggest the degree of entertainment appropriate, which was a great help in avoiding *faux pas*. Also friends from Lhasa stayed with us, like the Tarings and the Tsarongs, while en route to India to do shopping or to visit their children at school in Darjeeling. Raja and Rani Dorji from Kalimpong were regular visitors too. We entertained the members of the 1935 Everest Reconnaissance Expedition; I have a vivid memory of them all setting off down the garden with ice-axes and umbrellas, with those two great mountaineers, Eric Shipton and H. W. Tilman, carrying between them a wooden strong box full of cash to cover all the expedition's expenses. Frank Ludlow and George Sherriff were fairly frequent guests, and we also entertained that other great plant-hunter, Frank Kingdon Ward. Among our visitors in 1934 was Sir Charles Bell, who had done so much to foster good relations between Britain and Tibet when he had been P.O. Sikkim in the years around 1920. While Sir Charles spent three months in Tibet on a private visit, Lady Bell and their daughter Rongnye stayed with us in Gangtok. A rather more unusual visitor was a man named Stephen Smith, who at the time was pioneering a rather farfetched scheme for sending letters across Himalayan valleys by rocket. However, only one of his rockets managed to travel as far as a hundred yards ... And there were many more visitors—so many, in fact, that sometimes there barely seemed enough time to change the sheets between one set of visitors and the next.

Another of my responsibilities was to organize the servants, of whom we had quite a number. Some of them were employees of the Government of India and some were private servants, paid by us. Most of them could not speak a word of English and, as I for my part knew none of the local languages, I had to communicate by sign language.

Chief among the private servants was Samdup, Derrick's head manservant, who did speak English. Then there was Pinjo, our cook and the baker of all our bread. He had been employed at the Residency since the time of Colonel and Mrs. Eric Bailey. Pinjo's great weakness, as I have already described, was alcohol, but in fact he never let us down. He was by nature a very kind and lovable person, as one particular incident bears out.

One day I said to him: 'I'm tired of eating chicken and yak-meat and mutton, Pinjo. Wouldn't it be nice to have a duckling?'

Pinjo did not say anything at the time but, sure enough, we did have duckling for dinner that night. Then at the end of the week when I came to settle up with him (he was always scrupulously honest), he put at the bottom of his little account: 'One duckling—present from Pinjo.'

Pinjo was the only servant whose payment was entrusted to me; all the others were paid by the office, including the chaprassys who, although they were government employees, also did some work for us about the house and so received a little extra. The clerks were also government employees but the *dhobi* (washerman), was our own man, as was the driver of the car.

Our head table-man was Piangti; he used to serve our

food. Once a month I got him to lay out all the silver. I knew that I did not need to count it all up but I thought it just as well to let him know that I was keeping in touch with everything. All in all during the whole time that I was at the Residency, we only lost one dessert spoon, and my suspicion is that this was stolen by the servant of one of our visitors.

In December 1934, Sir Aubrey Metcalfe, the Foreign Secretary of the Government of India, and Lady Metcalfe stayed with us. On that occasion, I gave strict instructions to Piangti: 'Now, when you take up their morning tea, Piangti, be sure to use the best morning tea set.'

Piangti bowed. 'Yes, Memsahib.'

I thought no more about it. Later, however, I found out to my great amusement that he had taken up the heavy silver service—silver pot, silver hot water jug and everything else, all carried on a silver tray.

And then there were the *malis*, (gardeners). There were six in all, working under a head-mali named Ashi. Once I had an important garden-party planned and the day before I went out to inspect the garden; to my horror I found the malis planting flowers in the most incredibly rotten soil. I sent for Samdup without further ado. 'Will you please explain to Ashi that they must undo all the beds on the top terrace. Right at the top of the compound there is the most wonderful leaf-mould soil. They are to fill the beds with that,' I told him. 'They can have as many coolies as they want but it must all be done before tomorrow.'

Immediately Samdup had relayed the message, Ashi burst into floods of the most heart-rending tears.

'Good gracious!' I exclaimed to Samdup. 'What have I said?'

'Nothing, Memsahib,' Samdup replied. 'Those are tears of joy. For four years nobody has shown the slightest interest in the garden. Now Ashi sees that you are really interested, he is so moved that he cannot hold back his tears.'

A short while afterwards, Ashi sent word that they did not have enough flowers to plant the final bed.

'Up at the top of the compound there are masses of lovely foxgloves of many different colours,' I said. 'Ask him to make the bed of those. If they first of all dig little holes, then pour in a bucket of water into each and finally insert the plants, making absolutely sure to bed them down carefully, then I'm sure we'll have a marvellous show tomorrow.' And we did.

One day before a dinner-party was due to start, I went into the dining-room to check that the table had been properly laid and discovered that our large *cloisonné* incense-burner had been placed in the middle of the table with masses of bright red geraniums sticking up out of it to a height of eighteen inches! This meant that the guests sitting on one side of the table would have no chance of seeing those on the other side! In those days I had a small bed of violets just outside my own office, so I picked some of these. I then found one of a set of diamond-shaped bowls I had had brought up from Calcutta and made a little arrangement of violets in that. I also got out a set of candlesticks and some green candles.

When all was ready, I sent salaams to Ashi. When he came, I said: 'Well, Ashi—what do you think of that?'

He bowed. 'Bahut accha! Memsahib,' he replied. (Bahut accha means 'Very good' in Hindi)

'Now that you can see what I want, please get the other bowls ready for tonight.' I said.

Ashi had very touching little ways of expressing his gratitude for the interest I took in his work. For instance, he used to ask the dhobi the colour of the dress that he was pressing for me for that evening. Then, when I went up to the bedroom, I would find a little matching floret waiting for me on my dressing-table.

Ashi gave us excellent service and the grounds at the Residency looked magnificent under his care. On returning from our tours, I looked forward to seeing how the gardens had fared during our absence and what new blooms had appeared. I was never disappointed. We spent quite a lot on those gardens, rather more than the Government grant ran to, but it was well worth it for they gave us immense pleasure.

But fate later dealt a cruel blow to Ashi. He injured his leg and afterwards gangrene set in. There was nothing for it then but to amputate.

One day I said to Derrick: 'Do you think it would be a good idea if I went round to visit the servants in their own quarters every now and again?' And a good idea it turned out to be. On my very first visit, just as I came over the little hillock that hid the servants' quarters from the main house, I heard the most awful screaming. I rushed forward only to find that a poor child had been scalded with boiling oil. I called Dr. Hendricks at once and he saw to it that the child was properly treated.

After a time I think the servants actually came to appreciate my little visits. They demonstrated our active concern for them. We for our part always deeply appreciated their loyal help and support. Without it, we certainly could not have functioned properly. Needless to say, we were treated with unvarying respect by our servants. Serious insubordination was unheard-of. We knew that they regarded us as very exalted beings, but we were amazed when we found out exactly *how* exalted they believed us to be. They could not, for instance, credit that Derrick himself had sahibs above him. This misconception also applied to the local people, even to the Maharaja himself, who would not accept that the Foreign Secretary to the Government of India was Derrick's superior.

I also had to oversee the general running of the Residency. On the ground floor besides the large L-shaped drawing room with its two fireplaces and the two offices, one for Derrick and one for myself, there was a large hall with a dining-room off it and beyond that what I used to call the Tibetan Suite. Like all the bedrooms upstairs, this had its own bathroom and dressing-room.

Out in the grounds, besides the little cottage, there were servants' quarters and stables where our hill ponies were kept. There was also a tennis court. Derrick and I were both keen tennis players, though you had to be up early if you wanted a game because later a strong wind blew up and then play was virtually impossible. A kitchen garden attached to the Residency provided us with fresh vegetables. Other supplies could be obtained from the bazaar in Kalimpong. The local bazaar in Gangtok was rather small; sugar and flour could be bought there but not much else.

I ordered the main provisions from the Army & Navy Stores in Calcutta. This happened only once a year and was preceded by an elaborate stocktake. It had to be done carefully because it became very expensive to order anything separately. I set up a new system whereby Samdup made a note in a book every time he took something out of the godown, so that when it came to reordering all that needed to be done was to look in the book to see how much of everything we had left.

In my weekly routine, I always set Tuesday aside for writing letters home because that was the day the mail went. I made great efforts to write long and informative letters so that our families could share as fully as possible with me the wonderful experiences I was having. I in return was always pleased for news of what was happening at home.

In the evenings, our day's duties done, Derrick and I were often able to relax in the drawing-room. Sometimes we would just sit and read, he smoking his pipe, I knitting. I did a lot of knitting in those days and would never have dreamt of buying any woollen garments. At other times we played bridge. Derrick was a good player, as was Rai Bahadur Norbhu. I was not as skilful, but enjoyed playing.

We spent at least two evenings a week working on our cinema films and photographs. The films needed much editing as a lot of the footage was either under- or over-exposed. To do this we had to put in a special request for the electricity supply to be left on at full power until midnight. In those days electricity was generated from a small flume in Gangtok and, not being very powerful, current was switched down at

10.30 p.m. We mounted our many still photographs in great leather-bound albums, which are a complete pictorial record of our life and travels together. Derrick was a good photographer. He noted down every snap in a series of small notebooks, so it was easy to trace any negative that might be required. Of all Derrick's many photographs, I very much like a fine study that he made while he was Consul-General in Kashgar. This shows one of the local men holding a gigantic hunting eagle. Another photograph, which we particularly treasured was one Derrick had taken of the Dalai Lama in the gardens of the Chense Lingka, the only informal photograph ever taken of the 13th Dalai Lama.

Derrick liked music, mainly light classical, in particular the works of Gilbert and Sullivan. I vividly remember dashing down to Calcutta with him for a single night—we had no permit, so could not stay longer—to see a performance of one of the Savoy operas. He also liked to play the gramophone, particularly when working on his files in the mornings. He had numerous albums of records. Both gramophone and records used to go along with us on tour and in the remoter regions were regarded as miraculous, even magical, devices.

My great friend Chuni (Rani Dorji) and I had a hair-raising experience on one occasion when we were returning to Gangtok from Kalimpong by car. The driver, overcome by the heat of the valley, dozed off at the wheel and the car's two wheels went right off the road. The vehicle came to rest hanging half over a precipitous drop. We dared not even try to get out, as the slightest movement might have caused it to fall right over, so we stayed put until help arrived. The car was lashed to some trees for safety and only then were we assisted out. Chuni taught me how to eat mangoes without spilling the juice while we watched the car being set back on the road; then we resumed our journey.

While in Gangtok, we saw a good deal of the Sikkimese royal family. The Maharaja liked nothing better than to come to the Residency for a quiet dinner and on many occasions entertained us at his Palace. I remember very clearly Derrick and I lunching with him on *mo-mos*, which are small dumplings filled with minced meat. They are also very slippery and so I watched with admiration as the Maharaja dealt with his with great dexterity, just picking them up with his chopsticks one by one and popping them into his mouth.

'Well, that looks simple enough,' I thought to myself.

I could not have been more mistaken. My very first mo-mo, far from travelling obediently from my plate to my mouth, shot wilfully out of my chopsticks and went sliding across the highly polished floor.

The Maharaja was very kind, however, 'It's really quite easy,' he explained. 'You just catch each mo-mo at the back and then slip it quickly into your mouth. Try again . . .'

I followed his instructions and before long was quite expert in this particular gastronomic art.

We tended to see rather less of the Maharani than we did of the Maharaja, for in early May of 1934 she left Gangtok for Tibet on an extended pilgrimage and to visit her relations in Lhasa.

And so passed those happy days of our life at the Residency, up in the cool hills, high above the heat and dust of the sultry plains of India.

10 Sakya

As POLITICAL OFFICER in Sikkim, Derrick was expected to pay regular visits to the British Trade Agency in Gyantse. On our way there in 1934 we decided to visit Sakya and Shigatse. At first, we feared the sudden death of His Holiness might cause the Tibetan Government to withdraw the special permission the Dalai Lama had given us, but in the event they honoured it.

We were particularly excited at the prospect of visiting Sakya as no European had previously been allowed to visit that famous monastery. So, we started our journey in the second week of June 1934.

Sakya was a great monastic centre, lying about seventy miles west of Shigatse on the main trade route linking the Kathmandu valley of Nepal with the prosperous Shigatse region. Further to the west lie the upper reaches of the Tsangpo and western Tibet, an inhospitable region traditionally the domain of nomadic herders whose flocks provide plentiful wool and butter. The site of Sakya was considered a particularly auspicious one by the founder of the Sakya order of Tibetan Buddhism, Könchog Gyalpo (1034–1102), who established a monastery there in 1073 on land acquired from the local ruler. The choice seems to have been a fortunate one, for thereafter the order flourished both spiritually and temporally.

The great Mongol Emperor of China, Kublai Khan, became very interested in Tibetan Buddhism and made the Sakya Lama Phagpa (1235–80) his religious tutor as well as appointing him vassal ruler over Tibet. For the next century the Sakya Lamas were virtual kings of Tibet and the power and wealth of the Sakya monastery and its order increased accordingly. This was the start of the unusual 'patron and priest' relationship between Tibet and China, whereby the foremost Lama became religious adviser to the Emperor in return for patronage and protection in his role as secular ruler of Tibet. This relationship became strained during the present century when the Chinese tried to exercise direct control over Tibet. As the power of the Mongol dynasty in China waned, they became unable to continue their protection of the Sakya Lamas, who after about 1350 ceased to exercise temporal power in Tibet.

A distinctive feature of the Sakya order was the way in which the succession passed down from one head of the order to the next. Instead of a system based on reincarnation, as is used for the Dalai Lama lineage, a hereditary one was employed. A few generations before the time of our visit, however, the ruling family had split into two branches and the succession passed, not directly from father to son, but obliquely, from uncle to nephew.

For the first leg of our tour to Sakya we travelled slowly through the mountainous terrain of northern Sikkim. Our mainly uphill march along tracks that were often very hard going took us up the Lachung valley to Yumthang and the Dongkya pass.

Although it was very hot and sticky on the first day out, the temperature fell steadily as we progressed so that by the time we reached Lachung on the fourth day it was down to 60°F. The monsoon was then upon us, it rained a great deal and the swollen streams gushed noisily along their boulder-strewn beds. We saw many spectacular waterfalls, including one that was at least 200 feet high.

On 19 June, a misty, rainy day, we began to climb in earnest towards the high passes. The ponies tackled the rough road with spirit. We managed to find a sheltered place for our camp but next morning our tents, and all the ground about them, were covered with snow. The sky was clear though and we feasted our eyes on the mountains that surrounded us before clouds again swirled round them. Thereafter we only caught momentary glimpses of the peaks.

We were met five miles from Dobtra, a small village with a ruined dzong, by the Taring Raja (Jigme's father) and his second son, Chime. The Raja had a large estate here which was nominally the property of his half-brother, the Maharaja of Sikkim. Unfortunately in 1930 a terrible row had broken out between them over the estate and the Maharaja cut off the allowance he had been paying to the Raja. A short time before our visit Derrick had managed to smooth things over and persuade the Maharaja to restore the allowance.

We were put up in a pleasant three-roomed house which had been specially cleared out and prepared for us. Above the doorway a small wooden plaque bore the inscription: 'Sikkim Dak Bungalow, Doptra, 1927'—which was a little odd as we were a long way from Sikkim by this time; deep in Tibetan territory, in fact.

We spent the following day at Dobtra as guests of the Raja. After a latish breakfast, he and Derrick rode off with Chime to look over the estate. They covered about twenty miles and passed through several quite prosperous-looking villages of some six or eight houses each, but saw no trees bar those that had been planted in gardens. At one point, the Raja produced some quite remarkable Tibetan maps in order to point out the areas under dispute in the grazing controversy.

We left Dobtra on 25 June and travelled the remaining fifty-six miles to Sakya in three fairly easy stages. On the last day, having splashed through a waterlogged plain for about three miles and passed a ruined village, another village perched high up on the rocks caught our attention. The houses were painted slate-grey or white and were decorated with red, white or grey vertical stripes, a most unusual feature. Apparently the slate-grey houses belonged to devotees of the Sakya monastery while the white ones to the devotees of Shigatse. Later while climbing a bad road towards the Drimo-la (17,600 feet), we met a monk and his servant and a party of nuns going on a pilgrimage. Beyond the pass, going downhill again, we met a caravan of donkeys from Nepal bound for Lhasa with a cargo of paper.

The customary reception committees appeared as we drew near to Sakya, bearing katas and kind words of greeting. The head of the order, the Sakya Trizin, sent three representatives, two fifth-rank lay officials and a monk; but even before we met them, not far beyond the Drimo-la, we had encountered the splendidly attired representatives of his nephew and heir, the young Rinpoché. These consisted of a monk official in a gold papier mâché hat accompanied by a fine-looking syce wearing a decorative *soksha* (a Mongolian hat worn by secretaries and other assistants to high officials and dignitaries), colossal earrings studded with turquoises and a black chuba bound firmly around the waist with a red sash; a piece of leopard skin and two embossed silver plaques hung on each side. These two officials presented katas and enquired whether we would like to stay at the young Rinpoché's garden residence or prefer to camp; we preferred to camp.

Later, another monk official sent by the young Rinpoché arrived to escort us. Soon after meeting him, we turned to our right and Sakya itself swung into view. The first glimpse I caught was of a number of chörtens and then a large, low building, very squarely built and slate-grey in colour except for a band of red around the top of its walls. This was the principal temple on the south side of the shallow and narrow Yarlung river; it was known as the Hlochode Lhakang. The town itself extended up the hillside on the opposite bank of the river. It housed perhaps 3,000 or 4,000 people. All the houses were painted in the same picturesque striped manner that we had noticed earlier, while against the skyline there were more chörtens and the gilded roofs of many temples. The local people eagerly turned out to watch us riding in. On enquiry we discovered that only one other European had visited Sakya within living memory, a man called Hazard of the 1924 Everest Expedition, who had arrived without permission and had spent two or three days in the area making maps.

Turning south, we rode past the Sakya Trizin's potrang and on to the small walled garden that the young Rinpoché had kindly put at our disposal. It was too small to serve as our campsite, however, so after enjoying an open-air lunch of sausage and mash under its willows, we proceeded to an adjoining field, and it was in this pleasant spot that our tents were pitched alongside the brightly coloured Tibetan ones lent us by the young Rinpoché. The guide who had been assigned to us by Sakya Trizin was wearing one of the most extraordinary hats I have ever seen; a silk Homburg of a delicate shade of lavender, with a salmon-pink band.

About three o'clock that afternoon we received a call from the young Rinpoché. Derrick thought this a sign of great friendliness as normally one in his position did not come to make a first call himself but would wait to be called on first. He brought with him about twenty-five villagers, who advanced towards us singing and dancing. All were wearing their 'Sunday best' and the women wore the elaborate semi-circular Gyantse head-dresses.

The young Rinpoché turned out to be a comparatively tall man of about thirty-five, with expressive eyes set in a some-what skull-like face. Despite his status as next in line to the head of the order, there was little that was ascetic about him. He did not shave his head but wore his hair in a long plait. He wore a fine Chinese silk robe of a subtle shade of ivory, with a yellow shirt beneath that. A richly embroidered piece of cloth and a red silk shawl were wrapped around his shoulders.

After leaving us presents of grain, rice, eggs and mutton, the young Rinpoché temporarily withdrew so that Sakya Trizin's chief lay officer could present the official respects of the Sakya 'Government'.

Later, the young Rinpoché returned, bearing us a fine Tibetan meal of *thugpa* (noodles), meats and vegetables. He also brought his own chair, an old-fashioned plush affair of mid-Victorian design. He chatted to Derrick about Tsarong Dzasa, whose estates lay near by and who was well known to both of them, then he leant forward and asked Derrick to take his photograph the next day. He wanted to send the picture to the Prince of Torgut, a great friend, now returned to Turkestan.

We told the young Rinpoché how the Prince had called on us in Lhasa in 1933 to ask Derrick's advice as to whether it was safe to return to his home in northern Chinese Turkestan, in view of the troubles there. Derrick had advised him to delay his return and await the turn of events, but the Nechung Oracle had advised otherwise and he had started on his homeward journey. A few miles outside Lhasa, however, while cleaning his revolver, he had shot himself in the leg and, having returned to Lhasa rather shamefacedly, had told Derrick that he was a much better Oracle than the one at Nechung! The young Rinpoché was much amused.

We went to bed in a howling gale which blew itself out overnight. Our first visit next morning was to Sakya Trizin and his potrang. We were led through one courtyard, then another and finally conducted along a labyrinth of dark passageways until we reached his room. There we found an elderly man in his early sixties, well preserved but with trembling hands and unusually long fingernails. His dress was similar to that of the young Rinpoché. He received us seated and we were given chairs facing him. His twenty-five-year-old son sat on his right. Sakya Trizin's wife, the Gya-yum Kusho, was not present due to ill health, nor was the son's wife.

After having been given tea, rice and sweets, we presented our gifts, then Derrick and Sakya Trizin talked. The Sakya Trizin asked after our health and, having made sure that we were being well looked after, also asked to have his photograph taken, but not today as the local astrologers had decided that it would be inauspicious. The next day would have to do instead.

Sakya Trizin blessed all our servants, one by one, except for a Hindu sweeper who did not prostrate to the Lama.

We left to visit the town, accompanied by a monk and our friend, the gentleman in the lavender silk Homburg. We visited a few small temples and then crossed the river to take a look at the Hlochode Lhakang, the main temple. This had two outer courtyards, the larger of which was covered with wire netting and graced with truly enormous statues of the Guardian Kings of the Four Quarters. We found a ceremony in progress when we entered the main assembly hall. The monks wore greenish-yellow or red robes over their ordinary clothes and were sitting on rows of bodens about two and half feet high – about five times the usual height. There were several large and beautiful images and a number of chörtens containing the remains of former Sakya Trizins. It was too dark to see them clearly but they appeared to be made of wood covered with highly-embossed brass casing. The lineage could be traced back through fifty or sixty incarnations.

Behind the chörtens were literally thousands of sacred texts piled right up to the roof. Tibetan books are quite different from ours. They consist of loose sheets, about a foot or more long and a few inches wide, pressed between two heavy boards and wrapped in silk. This library was one of the most famous in Tibet and all its books were said to be hand written rather than printed from wooden blocks.

But what fascinated us most of all here were the gigantic tree trunks, about three feet in diameter, that served as pillars. Trees are rare enough in the barren wastes of Tibet, but trees of this size are non-existent except perhaps in the extreme south-eastern provinces. One of the pillars was said to have come from China, another from India, and two more from Tibet itself. The origins of the remainder were unknown.

The braying of great ten-foot trumpets greeted us as we approached the young Rinpoché's potrang. His syces ran out to greet us, accompanied by a small band and we walked the last few yards preceded by a man carrying a bunch of peacock feathers. When we were shown into the young Rinpoché's room, we found his wife was with him. This quiet but friendly lady was wearing beautiful brocades and the most elaborate head-dress I had ever seen. She seemed to be a little older than her husband. We handed over our gifts and then, after taking tea, adjourned to the cleaner of the two outer courtyards for photography. The young Rinpoché insisted on posing for the camera in an assortment of clothes and with various groupings of his family, including his six-year-old son. The whole family later had lunch with us at our camp, including Sakya Trizin's son. They found European food too unfamiliar and ate little.

After lunch our visitors examined our tents and other possessions in minute detail and were particularly taken with my travelling bathroom. We played the gramophone for them and they departed at about four o'clock, inspecting the kitchen and store tents as they left. They returned a couple of hours later, bearing farewell presents, which included an attractive charmbox, two pairs of stirrup irons and a bridle, some brick tea and sugar cane. They stayed for about an hour and during that time told us a great deal about the Sakya order.

One story they told us was about the corpse of a long-dead Sakya Trizin. It was kept in the present Sakya Trizin's room at Sakya and beautiful flowers bloomed amid the bones; something I actually saw for myself. As I sat in our tent listening to their captivating story with the hurricane lamp casting an unstable light upon the oriental faces of our visitors, I wondered whether it was all a dream. As a farewell gift we presented our guests with a clock. They had never owned one before and we had to teach them how to wind it up and set the hands. We gave the young Rinpoché's wife three cakes of soap, which was what we were told she would like.

Next day, after exchanging more presents, we went to take Sakya Trizin's photograph as arranged. We found him with his attendants waiting for us in one of the courtyards of his potrang. The Sakya Trizin, wearing a tall red cap, was seated on a throne; his attendants stood, looking wonderful in their sumptuous official costumes. Afterwards there was tea and rice, then we took our leave with the usual exchange of katas. Our servants were given blue blessing strips of silk to be worn round their necks until they dropped off.

We were finally seen off from Sakya by six officials, who rode out with us for the first mile and a half. We then proceeded on a long march of some twenty-six miles to the country domain of our Anglophile friend, Tsarong Dzasa, of whom we had seen a great deal in Lhasa the year before. Unfortunately, while Derrick and I were enjoying such pleasant tranquillity in this interesting and little-known quarter of Tibet, away in Lhasa ominous developments were taking place.

11 Shigatse and Gyantse

AFTER LEAVING SAKYA, we crossed two high passes and encountered steep and stony places where the going was hard; we also, by contrast, traversed a green, well-cultivated valley before coming at length into the country domain of Tsarong. Tsarong himself was away in Lhasa at the time; he had returned there on 28 May after having wisely kept his distance during the preceding power struggle. In early July he took over Kunphel-la's old post as Director of Trapchi. In his absence, we were greeted on his behalf by his steward and headman, who rode out with tea and chang. In their company we rode downhill to Tsarong's country house, which lay near a river with a bright green expanse of cultivation surrounding it; also many willow and poplar trees.

The house was of the usual Tibetan design but far larger and grander than any other house in the region. It possessed an outer courtyard of parade-ground proportions as well as an inner courtyard where we finally dismounted. While the ponies were led away to be stabled, we were taken up to the second floor of the house, which consisted of three large rooms and a fine kitchen. Our tour clerk, Gyaltsen, had his own room on the same floor and the kitchen was situated here too. Usually we avoided lodging in Tibetan houses unless we could be confident that they were reasonably free of fleas!

As we were settling in, Tsarong's steward presented himself and handed Derrick a small bag sealed with Tsarong's seal, which contained the keys to the house.

Later that day a dramatic thunderstorm raged. Ominous rumbling broke overhead and the dark sky was from time to time brilliantly lit by jagged veins of lightning, while at the same time rain and hail were hurled down upon the tile roof of the house. After it was all over there were a few minutes of calm; then we were startled by a loud noise coming from across the valley. I joined Derrick at the window. Half an hour previously the far hillside had been just arid rock; now a great cataract of water was cascading down it. Already about 600 feet long and growing longer every second, it tumbled over ledge after ledge until it finally reached the river far below. It gushed at full spate for about five minutes and then began to slacken off, eventually vanishing as abruptly at it had begun.

Next morning I began our day at Tsarong by writing some letters home and catching up with my diary. Then Derrick and I took the keys and went with the steward to look over the house. The ground floor consisted of stables in the main; the first floor was a warren of storerooms and servants' quarters; the principal rooms were on the second floor, where we were staying; finally, the top floor was given over to shrine-rooms.

The top floor interested us the most, especially the Gön-khang, the room where the deities who guarded the house were reputed to live. I felt a little apprehensive as we entered, but all we found were guns and thangkas and a few masks. We went into a large hall and were delighted, on opening an interesting looking chest, to find that we had found the Tsarong family's collection of thangkas. There were three in particular that we found very beautiful; two large appliqué ones and a tiny example executed in the most exquisite embroidery.

WE LEFT TSARONG ON 1 JULY for our next objective, Shigatse, the second city of Tibet.

As we dropped towards the city, the great monastic complex of Tashilhunpo gradually came into view. It was a large, rambling place, about the size of Sera near Lhasa, only more impressive, extending along the lower slopes of a hillside rising from the plain. Near it was a fine dzong, a kind of miniature Potala, and in the distance the flashing waters of the great Tsangpo river could just be glimpsed.

A mile from Shigatse we were given ceremonial tea and rice in a grand tent that had been pitched in our honour by the acting head of the Tashilhunpo Government. A great crowd of villagers—mostly old ladies—surrounded the tent while we were being entertained in it. We then went on to camp in a rather damp lingka with a dilapidated house attached to it.

In camp I noticed that Samdup, Derrick's factotum, looked deeply depressed.

'What's the matter, Samdup?' I asked.

He said nothing, just thrust a letter into my hand. He had received it with the other mail that had reached us at Natang earlier in the day. I quickly read it and learnt that Paktu, Samdup's eight-and-a-half month old daughter, had died at Yatung. Derrick and I both shared Samdup's distress, for Paktu had been a fine baby and had only been ill for two days.

Tashilhunpo monastery was founded in 1445, reputedly by Gendun-drup, the nephew of Tsongkhapa, founder of the Gelugpa tradition of Tibetan Buddhism. The heads of Tashilhunpo had for centuries been the line of Panchen Lamas. Unfortunately, during the eighteenth century, the Chinese had attempted to offset the growing power of the Dalai Lamas in Lhasa by building up that of the Panchen Lamas, who were given powers to govern Tsang province. This inevitably produced friction between Lhasa and Tashilshunpo and eventually culminated in the flight of the Panchen Lama in 1923. In his absence, the Lhasa Government appointed an official of the third rank, the Dzasa Lama, to be in charge of his domains. This man was therefore head of the so-called Tashilhunpo Government during the time of our visit and he was nominally superior to the two local dzongpöns or district governors, although these too received direct instructions from Lhasa.

The town of Shigatse itself was a large one by Tibetan

standards with a population in the region of 10,000. It was situated on a flat plain to the south-west of the junction of the Nyang and Tsangpo rivers. The houses, quite a number of which were of stone, were well built, but the low-lying situation of the place made it far less impressive as a town than, say, Gyantse.

On our first day in Shigatse, 3 July, we stayed in camp and received some fourteen callers, the most important of whom was the Dzasa Lama. He turned out to be over sixty with a bald head and a small goatee beard that made him look the very epitome of a wise sage. He was most polite and earnestly enquired whether we had everything necessary for our comfort. He had apparently held his appointment for about nine years and was well liked, which we could well understand from the impression he made on us.

The next morning, by good fortune a fine one, we returned the Dzasa Lama's call at his private house just below the monastery. We took breakfast and afterwards presented him with gifts. As we were leaving, all the usual formalities having been duly observed, he thrust a jar of barley sugar drops into my hands, saying in Tibetan to Derrick as he did so that he felt I would need to have something to sustain me while sightseeing.

The Dzasa Lama's senior assistant, the Khenchung or Junior Abbot, showed us around Tashilhunpo, which we were told housed about 3,000 monks. This meant that it was not as large as either Drepung or Sera, but it was much more interesting. It consisted of a maze of buildings with narrow, cobbled alleyways running between them. From the outside I was particularly struck by the many gilded roofs and the towering blank wall upon which a giagantic thangka was hung on one supremely auspicious day each year. Our guide conducted us through numerous shrine and chörten rooms and assembly halls, all rather dark, grimy and smelling of rancid butter, but also richly endowed with all manner of priceless hangings, paintings and images. We were also shown the empty throne of the absent Panchen Lama.

(Previous page) Maharaja and Maharani of Bhutan in Sikkim.

Monk with a large prayer wheel.

Looking South into Sikkim from the Chak-la.

(Following page) Twin peaks and lake in Northern Sikkim.

North face of Kanchenjau.

(Opposite) Maharaja and Maharani of Bhutan and entourage in Calcutta. Seated: Rani Dorji, Derrick, Maharani, Maharaja, self, Raja Dorji. In front: Crown Prince Jigme and Ashi Kesang Dorji (later to be King and Queen of Bhutan).

The 1935 Mount Everest party at the Residency.

Samdup, Phagmo and baby.

An old Lepcha.

Maharani of Bhutan with Crown Prince Jigme at Calcutta Zoo.

(Opposite) Monk band at Tumlong Monastery.

The Panchen Lama.

In one gompa we found a small army of monks sitting on rows of high bodens with huge books before them from which they were chanting. They wore yellow cloaks. We also inspected the great kitchens in which the tea was made. Seven gigantic cauldrons were being boiled over roaring fires. They were emptied four times a day, every monk receiving two cups at each serving, for which the sixty copper kettles we saw in a passageway were used. The tea was the Chinese brick variety, churned with butter, salt and soda.

Later we were conducted to the printing shops where shelf after shelf of carved wooden blocks were stored. One was taken down and the method used in printing demonstrated for our benefit. Ink was taken from a jug and rubbed onto the carved top surface of the block, then a clean sheet of rough, fibrous local paper was placed on it and rubbed with a roller. The printed sheet was then peeled off and presented to me. I accepted it gratefully and preserved it as a memento of my visit.

We saw much else besides on our first visit to Tashilhunpo but were particularly struck by the numerous fine thangkas, most of which were painted in gouache upon canvas, though a few were of appliqué or embroidery. Derrick and I had already managed to acquire some good thangkas during our travels and had begun to develop a taste for them, so we naturally cast envious eyes over these ancient and no doubt priceless ones. We also saw many fine images: in one room alone there were 3,000.

We would have liked to have been able to linger and examine all the wonders of this vast ancient treasure house at our leisure but duty obliged us to leave at about noon and proceed to the house of the Western Dzongpön, where we were expected for lunch. After that we were scheduled to visit the Eastern Dzongpön for a second lunch!

We were able to return to Tashilhunpo briefly the next morning to continue our sightseeing tour and were shown the sacred tombs of some of the earliest Panchen Lamas. These consisted of a number of individual chörtens, each of which had its own shrine surmounted by a splendid gilded roof. Many butter lamps burned in each shrine, giving off the by now unmistakable odour. This remarkable sight was outdone, however, by something else we saw that day, one of the minor wonders of the world: a colossal statue of Maitreya, the Coming Buddha, some seventy to eighty feet high. It had been commissioned by the present exiled Panchen Lama and no less than nine flights of steps went up past it to the roof.

DURING OUR TOUR OF SOUTHERN TIBET that year the activities of the Chinese were seldom far from Derrick's thoughts and he awaited news from Lhasa with keen anticipation.

The fall of Lungshar in May 1934 had brought to an end the dramatic period of power struggle that had troubled Lhasa following the death of the Thirteenth Dalai Lama; and Tibet had begun to stabilize politically under the steady rule of the Regent's government. Almost at once, however, that government was put to the test by a new crisis which effectively thwarted any hope of a return to a peaceful existence. This time the menace came from without and from a traditional quarter: China.

In the early months of 1934, well before we set off on tour, Derrick had begun to receive disquieting reports of developments in China. In January, General Huang Mu-sung, a Vice Chief of Staff, was formally appointed Special Commissioner for Ceremonial Offerings to the late Dalai Lama. Ostensibly his function was to proceed to Tibet and offer condolences to the Tibetan people. From the start, however, realists suspected that the real object of this Mission of Condolence was to pave the way for a renewal of Chinese power in Tibet.

Huang himself took many months to reach Lhasa travelling overland from China, but in the meantime an Advance Party was sent on ahead by sea to prepare the way for him. Thus two sinister figures, William Tsiang and L.M. Wang, arrived in India from China, travelling on British diplomatic visas. They brought staff with them—and extensive luggage.

In April they passed through Kalimpong, where they met our friend Tobgye (Raja Dorji), who informed Derrick that he was not impressed either with the men themselves, who seemed neither intelligent nor energetic, or with their open boasts of the lavish presents and the large sums of cash that they were bringing to Lhasa. They expressed an interest in Derrick, however: was the Political Officer in Sikkim the kind of man who would consent to see them were they to pay him a visit? they wondered. I am glad to say they did not come to call on us but instead proceeded directly to Tibet, where they made good use of the British dak bungalows along the route to Lhasa. Derrick reported to his superior officers:

> I have heard from another source that they profess to be most impressed with the strength of our position in Tibet and the immense efforts that will be required to undermine it. This appears to indicate the real object of the mission.

Derrick did not go to Lhasa himself in 1934 but his Personal Assistant, Rai Bahadur Norbhu, arrived there on 25 April and remained, keeping a watchful eye on all developments and reporting back frequently, until the end of the year. He was thus able to inform us of the arrival of the Chinese Advance Party, which took place on 24 May. The Tibetans went out of their way to make the party welcome and were rewarded with rudeness: the Chinese failed to dismount or even stop their horses while the salute was being played.

News reached us at Shigatse concerning the activities of the Chinese Advance Party in Lhasa. They had apparently met the Regent, the Lönchen and the Shapés, and had been given a lunch by the Tibetan Government. By and large, however, the feeling among Tibetan officials seemed to be that 'while friendship with China would be excellent, domination by China would be very much the reverse'. In what was no doubt a carefully worked out plan to ingratiate themselves, the Chinese officials were lavish in their distribution of presents and cash: Norbhu reported that $50,000 had been distributed to the great monasteries of Lhasa alone, so there was always the danger that the hearts and minds of monks and of high officials might be bought. 'This is, I fear, a very real danger,' Derrick wrote in one of his reports; he also stressed the importance of Rai Bahadur Norbhu remaining in Lhasa for the time being, even though the Chinese were openly hostile towards him. They had, it seemed, denounced him to the Lönchen as a 'bad man' who, despite being of Tibetan origin himself, served the British Government.

Dewa Shar, on leave from his usual duties as Assistant Telegraph Master in Lhasa, reported to Derrick that the Chinese seemed to actively dislike all the boys who had received an English education, himself included. The people of Lhasa were becoming worried that these uninvited guests from China might never go away. Derrick was also most disquieted to hear that the Chinese had brought wireless equipment with them.

DESPITE WHAT WAS HAPPENING IN LHASA, we went on with the formalities of our visit to Shigatse. On 6 and 7 July we hosted two luncheon parties for local officials. About sixteen monk officials turned up for the first and the whole affair turned out to be rather hilarious. At one point in the proceedings, perhaps in order to liven things up a little, Derrick produced a bottle of *crème de menthe*, a drink for which the Tibetans had a particular liking. Afterwards, the tempo of the evening changed, peels of laughter were heard and there was much joking.

On 9 July we rode out of Shigatse, escorted for about a mile by various local officials and friends. It was a fine day and good to be on the move again, especially as the going was good. Our next destination was Gyantse, sixty miles away, and we travelled there in three easy stages.

We left Dongtse, our last halting place, at about 7.45 a.m. and in under two hours reached the Sechen Bridge. There our escort met us and accompanied us into Gyantse where we were to spend six weeks in the dak bungalow. A reception committee also arrived composed of the Dzongpöns, the Abbot and the Nepalese Agent in Gyantse; also a steward bearing a kata and greetings from the Taring Rani.

Gyantse and its surrounding countryside seemed much greener than the year before, but then we had not arrived until October, when the intense cold of the Tibetan winter was well set in. Now it was July and summer had not yet begun to wane.

Socially, the climax of our stay in Gyantse in 1934 was the great firework party we held at the Agency on 29 August. It was the talk of the town for several weeks. Everyone turned out to see our bonfire, which lit up the sky, while for an hour the peace of the Roof of the World was shattered by the bangs, whizzes, cracks and whirrings of our squibs, rockets, Catherine-wheels, crackers and other pyrotechnic marvels. The guest of honour was Dorje Phagmo, the Abbess of Samding monastery, a small, friendly woman of about forty with raven-black hair parted in the middle and fastened in a plait. She had travelled for two days to be present, bringing her nephew with her. Derrick and I had visited her at Samding monastery on our way back from Lhasa in the autumn of 1933 and were particularly pleased to see her again.

The town itself was rather empty; many important officials were away in Lhasa, where the Chinese menace still loomed large. The main body of the Chinese Mission of Condolence had still not arrived in Lhasa, but it now appeared that the senior members of the Advance Party were beginning to assert themselves. They had tried to raise the national flag over their house in Lhasa on more than one occasion and had even had the effrontery to suggest that, when their leader arrived, he should be accommodated in the Norbhu Lingka. They also wanted Tibetan officials to co-operate in laying on a lavish ceremonial welcome for the great man. They complained too about the Lhasa police's habit of marching daily through the city with their band playing 'Cock o' the North' and other British tunes. British music should not be played, they asserted, only Tibetan music. As if all this were not enough, they had also misbehaved in private; Derrick received reports of a fight breaking out between Tsiang and Wang over a woman and of crockery being thrown!

Throughout August, Norbhu was sending in reports as the main body of the Chinese Mission of Condolence got steadily closer to Lhasa. It finally arrived there on 28 August and various officials went a mile outside the city to greet its leader, Huang Mu-sung, so he did get the honourable welcome for which the Advance Party had been pressing—a more honourable welcome than had been accorded to Derrick himself as representative of the British Raj the previous year.

Another matter that was preoccupying Derrick at this time was the question of the return to Tibet of the exiled Panchen Lama. By 1934, the Tibetans had become very anxious to secure his return, not least perhaps because an oracle had predicted danger to his life. New conditions had been put to the Tibetan Government by his representatives, whom Derrick had met when they had passed through Kalimpong in March. But the new Tibetan Government were to prove themselves no more accommodating than the late Dalai Lama had been and rejected several of the Panchen Lama's demands. The Lama himself was not at all pleased when he got news of this and promptly dispatched another mission, which passed through Gyantse in July while we were there. The Panchen Lama now wanted the British to help arrange a solution, for he was eager to get back to Tashilhunpo himself. The British were prepared to do so on an informal basis but at this stage they did not want to become officially involved as they regarded the matter as essentially an internal one to Tibet. The whole issue was given special urgency when reports began to come through that the Panchen Lama had acquired many armed troops with whom he might be preparing to re-enter Tibet by force. Around him always lurked the Chinese menace, for they had unilaterally declared him to be the spiritual head of Tibet in the absence of a Dalai Lama and might always use him to further their own designs.

12 Into Bhutan Once More

WE LEFT GYANTSE on 4 September to make a detour into Bhutan so that we could spend a few days with our friend Tobgye (Raja Dorji). Our route now took us to Tuna, in three stages, across a bare and stony but still beautiful landscape. Our path ran for a time beside the Dochen lake, a sheet of clear blue water on the far side of which rose a range of snow-clad mountains, among them Chomolhari, regarded as sacred by the Tibetans. Its knife-edged ridges and peaks dominate the whole plain of Tuna with an awesome grandeur. It was cold as we climbed the eleven-mile incline up to the 15,200 foot Tang-la. That day, the higher reaches of Chomolhari appeared to hover above a band of cloud encircling its base. Beyond the pass the way was stony and the temperature dropped lower and lower.

Phari, our next port of call, has an atrocious reputation. Travellers have dubbed it the 'filthiest place on earth'—and not without justice, for rubbish has been dumped in its streets for many centuries, with the result that the level has been progressively raised. We were escorted into the town by the dzongpön who called on us later at the dak bungalow.

About half an hour after we had arrived in Phari, Dr. Hendricks, our GP from Gangtok, rode in from Gautsa. He, too, was to accompany us into Bhutan. A little later he was followed by Seng-ge, the Ha Dzongpön, and some of Togbye's servants, who had come to guide us over the frontier.

It was a great pleasure to see real trees again and to be in a damper climate once we had crossed into Bhutan the next day by way of the 17,000 foot Gya-la. Straightaway presents of vegetables and wild pig arrived for us, sent by Togbye. They were Togbye's yak that grazed on the green grass of the valley through which we passed on our way to our first Bhutanese campsite at Tsethangka. A heavy dew was glistening when we got up the next morning, a welcome change after the aridity of the Tibetan plateau. The last mile of the five-mile approcah to the Ya-la (17,500 feet) was so steep that we had to dismount and walk to the top. After this we dropped steeply, then climbed a second pass which gave us access to the Ha valley. We then descended to the river where we paused for an open air lunch before going on to Damthang where to our delight Togbye awaited us.

Togbye left us later that day to return to Ha. We followed him next morning, travelling about eight miles in gorgeous sunshine and beating for wild boar for the first mile. Tobgye met us about half a mile from Ha with a reception committee of nineteen tiny schoolboys.

'I'm sorry all these boys are so small,' he apologized. 'Unfortunately, the bigger boys had an argument with their schoolteacher and had to return to their homes.'

We spent twelve happy days in Ha and among other diversions, like archery and watching football and boxing matches, we managed to get in some shikar. This was a great privilege for at the time British subjects residing in Tibet or Sikkim were not allowed to freely pursue sport in Bhutanese territory. In fact, the authorities had recently lodged formal complaints about poachers, who were doing a great deal of damage to the game in Bhutan by their shooting and trapping. The British authorities responded by warning British subjects living within the limits of the Gyantse and Yatung trade marts that if they were caught poaching in Bhutan they would be liable to arrest and punishment under the laws of Bhutan.

But for Derrick, our stay in Ha was not all hunting and relaxation. Even in that high, remote and peaceful valley, news of the latest dramatic events in Lhasa still reached him, and he had to collate all the information he received and report back to his superiors.

It seemed that the leader of the Chinese Mission of Condolence, Huang Mu-sung, was going out of his way to make a good impression in Lhasa. He had visited or been visited by all the most influential Tibetans and was lavish in his entertaining. Cleverly he gave politics a wide berth, leaving it up to the Tibetans themselves to take the first initiative in broaching any unresolved questions. This they eventually did, specifically mentioning certain ongoing frontier problems but at the same time making it clear that they adhered strictly to the late Dalai Lama's position on Tibetan autonomy. Huang apparently dismissed these matters as trifles which could be easily settled, but coyly regretted that he had no authority to do so, his mandate being just to perform religious ceremonies. In view of his exalted rank, the Tibetan officials could not believe that he was as powerless as he pretended.

I was sad when at last the day came for us to leave Ha. We left the guest-house early and visited the local hospital. Then after an early lunch we went hunting. We camped again at Damthang that night and Tobgye honoured us by staying and playing bridge with us. Next day we said goodbye to Tobgye and his men, first exchanging katas, then both they and we rode our separate ways, waving our katas and calling until we could see each other no more.

Our nine days at Yatung passed pleasantly enough. I played tennis and bridge, watched hockey, visited the local hospital, school and post office and even tried a little target practice with Derrick's rifle. The outstanding social event was undoubtedly the entertainment that was put on by the clerks in the barracks one night. It was called *The Drama of King Harishchandra* and was a wonderfully overdone performance full of extravagant mythological characters.

Reports from Lhasa that Derrick received here suggested that relations between the Tibetans and their Chinese visitors were becoming tense. The Chinese had caused offence by smoking in the streets of Lhasa. During a visit to Sera monastery by their leader, Huang Mu-sung, the monks had displayed clear hostility by jostling the party. The Tibetan Government did agree, however, under pressure from Huang, to accept a seal he had brought with him for the late Dalai Lama, though earlier they had decided to refuse it. At the same time they agreed to accept an inscribed jade slab.

One small piece of secret information particularly interested Derrick. One of the telegraph messages the Chinese had sent home had, on being decoded, been found to contain unexpected words and phrases like 'heavy lubricating oil' and 'gasoline'. Presumably these were needed in connection with the new wireless transmitter that the Chinese had set up with the passive acceptance of the Tibetan Government.

Leaving Yatung on 7 October, it took us three marches to return to home base at Gangtok. Rain dogged us during the last two days, but it was cheering to be greeted about two miles from home by the usual reception committee, who had brought us chang, bananas and apples. A police band was there to welcome us at the Residency itself and all our friends were waiting inside. We had drinks together in the empty drawing room and afterwards set about the annual ritual of unpacking and putting the denuded house back in good order again.

One thing was then in the forefront of my mind. Before we'd left to go on tour I'd had a special word with Faquir Chand, the State Engineer of Sikkim. As we still had some Residency funds left I asked him to arrange to have Derrick's office panelled and a window-seat put in where Derrick could do his crossword.

'Now I must get into the office before the Sahib does so that I can see the look on his face,' I said to Samdup upon our return.

It was all well worth while. Derrick was delighted. 'This is magnificent,' he exclaimed when he came into the room and inspected the fine new woodwork.

There was a little surprise in store for me too. When I went into the dining-room I found fourteen one-pound tins of Firpo's chocolates on the table: a present from Derrick!

That night I wrote my last entry in my diary of that year's tour of Sikkim, Tibet and Bhutan: 'It's nice to be back and we've had a good tour.'

IMMEDIATELY AFTER OUR RETURN from tour, while I busied myself with domestic arrangements, Derrick was still pre-occupied with the situation in Lhasa.

In September had come news that Huang Mu-sung had presented his special seal and jade slab in ceremony at the Potala. He had made rich offerings and engaged a hundred monks to perform ceremonies at the tomb for a month. Shortly afterwards though he revealed his true intentions when he asked the Tibetan Government to declare a republic and admit that the Tibetan people were one of the so-called 'Five Races of China'. While the Tibetan Government were prepared to admit that a special relationship had long existed between the Tibetans and the Chinese, 'like two eyes', they could not comply with Huang's request, whereupon the situation began to get ugly. If the Tibetan Government could not co-operate, Huang intimated, then the Chinese Government would be unable to stop the Panchen Lama, who had joined the Chinese Republic himself and was now supported by a large number of armed troops, from returning to Tibet by force. He also tried to undermine the British position in Tibet by saying that China and Tibet were 'one family' and help from outsiders was not wanted.

Huang, though not highly regarded in official British eyes, nevertheless conducted himself with decorum while he was in Lhasa. Not so his subordinates. They not only failed to show due respect to their leader in public but offended the Tibetans by galloping wildly through the streets of Lhasa, getting drunk and quarrelling among themselves. The worst offender was apparently L.M. Wang of the Advance Party, who caused a near riot on one occasion and afterwards had to be carried back to his quarters insensible.

By November, Derrick was becoming concerned about the stratagems of one Wu Min-Yuan, a man who had been born in Lhasa but of mixed Chinese and Tibetan parentage. He now began to enact the first scenes of an elaborate charade that the Chinese had devised in the hope of achieving their main objectives. Wu claimed that the sensitive Huang had been cast into a deep depression by the stubborn refusal of the Tibetan Government to yield to his reasonable requests. He, Wu, therefore, in the hope of resolving the deadlock, had devised a set of fourteen articles. If the Tibetan Government would agree to these, then he was sure that hurt feelings would be assuaged and harmony restored.

The Tibetan Government still held firm, however. Some of the articles were more or less acceptable to them; others were not. On hearing their response, Huang quit his melancholy seclusion and began to press the Tibetan Government to accept the fourteen articles himself, laying particular stress on three points:

1. That Tibet should admit subordination to China;
2. That all direct communication with outside nations should cease, or, failing that, China should be consulted before the Tibetan Government replied to any communication with outside nations; and
3. That China should be consulted prior to the appointment of high ranking officials.

After lengthy discussion, the National Assembly decided that it would agree to recognize Chinese suzerainty—that is, its nominal authority over Tibet—but only on the conditions laid down at the Simla Conference of 1914, which guaranteed internal autonomy. As regards the second point, it was decided that Tibet would have to reserve the right to have direct dealings with outside nations, 'headed by the British'. Finally, as a friendly gesture, they conceded that they might inform the Chinese of the appointment of certain high officials—but only after the event. As a rider, the National Assembly expressed a desire that the British Government be a party to any agreement between China and Tibet.

The last point was totally unacceptable to Huang, who promptly returned home for discussions. He left Lhasa on 29th November, leaving behind two officials. The wireless and its operators also remained in Lhasa. These events caused deep concern in British official circles.

13   Bhutan Comes to Calcutta

DURING OUR FIRST visit to Bhutan in 1933, His Highness the Maharaja had told Derrick that he would like to visit Calcutta, following the example of his father who had been there in 1906. Winter was the most appropriate time for such a visit for at other seasons that busy city can be very hot or humid and as such, especially uncomfortable for people from the cooler, clearer climate of the hills. Arrangements were made for the visit to take place at the very end of 1934, extending a little into the new year, so no sooner were Derrick and I safely back from our 1934 tour than it was time to get ready for Calcutta.

Fortunately, Tobgye had matters already well in hand and had managed to rent a large property, number 42 Chowringhee, for two months. As soon as we could gain access, Chuni and I hurried to Calcutta to organize furniture and fittings, for the place was being let unfurnished, and to get everything in order. While Chuni and I were engaged in the interior of the house, Tobgye was organizing the construction of a whole village of wooden huts at the bottom of the garden. These were for the two hundred or so retainers who were to accompany the Royal party. When I was satisfied that all the preparations had been properly made, I returned to Gangtok.

Meanwhile, up in the high, green valleys of Bhutan, the Maharaja was also busily making preparations for his forthcoming visit. To date, His Highness had only once been outside Bhutan and then only as far as the Assam border district of Darrang. He had never seen a broad gauge train. The Maharani on the other hand, had not been outside her native country at all and had never even seen a bicycle.

Derrick and I went down to Jalpaiguri, where the narrow gauge joins the main railway line, to meet the train bringing the royal party from Hashimara. And what a splendid sight they were when they arrived! Their Highnesses wore colourful Bhutanese costumes, as did the more than two hundred retainers who accompanied them, each of whom was armed with bow and arrows and had a shield slung over his shoulder. After the official reception, it was back into the train and full steam ahead for Calcutta.

The dramatic contrast between the great modern metropolis of Calcutta, where we arrived at midday, and the simplicity and tranquillity of life in the hills was very apparent even to me – and I was after all well acquainted with modern urban life. How much more of an impact then must it make upon Their Highnesses. Would they feel overwhelmed by the hooting, speeding traffic, by the milling crowds kept in constant motion by the remorseless drives that activate the modern commercial world, by the sheer profusion of buildings, among them great administrative, business, religious and public edifices? I observed them both closely. They were certainly very interested and asked many intelligent questions, but they took it all in their stride.

Protocol demanded that Their Highnesses accompanied by Tobgye and Chuni, and Derrick and myself, should spend the first four nights at Government House as guests of Sir John Anderson, the Governor of Bengal. This allowed us time to explain a host of new and unfamiliar things to Their Highnesses; it also allowed the two hundred retainers time to install themselves at 42 Chowringhee.

At one early lunch hosted by Sir John Anderson, at which there were a hundred and twenty guests, Sir John turned to me and asked whether I would mind interpreting for the Maharani who, not being able to speak any English herself, was sitting in enforced silence on Sir John's right.

'I'm afraid I don't speak any Bhutanese myself,' I was forced to admit; 'but if you allow me to change places with Rani Chuni, I'm sure that she will be able to translate wonderfully for you.'

As soon as I'd spoken I realised that I had committed a terrible *faux pas* in suggesting a change of seating plan on such a formal occasion.

Fortunately Sir John took it in the spirit in which it was intended. 'Would you mind?' he said gallantly. 'Only in that it deprives me of the pleasure of sitting next to you,' I replied, and then feeling highly uncomfortable, I walked around that enormous table under the astonished stares of all the guests, all the men, including Sir John, having risen to their feet. Once we had exchanged places, I signalled to Chuni and we both sat down. Then Sir John leant across the table and said, 'Thank you very much', after which all the men sat down too. What an intense relief it was when lunch at last got under way!

As the Maharaja had expressed a desire to see 'everything,' I had previously written to Joan Townend, whose husband, Herbert, was one of the secretaries to Sir John Anderson. Joan knew everyone in Calcutta and was therefore well qualified to arrange a programme for the royal party. Two visits a day were planned for the first three weeks, allowing sufficient time for lunches and dinners. Joan came up trumps and organized a wonderful programme. Not a moment of Their Highnesses's time was wasted. They went to the Zoological Gardens, the Mint, the gun and shell factory at Cossipore, HMS *Emerald*, Tollygunge and the Victoria Memorial, to mention just a few visits. They also watched polo, saw an edition of *The Statesman* newspaper being printed on paper which His Highness said he had seen being made at the Titagarh paper mills that same morning. His Highness and some of his retainers went up in an aeroplane, and afterwards he agreed to become a patron of the Bengal Flying Club. Interspersed among all this were the inevitable lunches and dinners with diplomats, businessmen and civil servants.

It should be added that the royal party was considerably expanded by the arrival of the Maharaja of Sikkim and his family, who took over the entire top floor of the Grand Hotel and naturally wanted to be included in everything; several of our Tibetan friends also arrived.

The army of retainers brought from Bhutan thought that the Maidan, the great open space off Chowringee, would be an excellent place for an archery contest. Reports of this reached us one morning and caused Derrick no small alarm. People flocked all the time to this open space in the crowded city, but now there were more than ever, attracted no doubt by the colourful traditional costumes the Bhutanese were wearing. Moreover it is unlikely that these city dwellers had ever seen a bow and arrow before.

We managed to persuade these proud warriors from the Himalayas that, although archery contests were certainly appropriate in their native hills, they were really not quite the thing for busy modern cities. Graciously, they took down their targets and withdrew.

The races each Saturday were a time of well-earned relaxation for several of us. Tobgye had a string of horses in Calcutta so, for him, these were not events of merely academic interest. On one occasion, while he was cheering one of his own horses, he felt a hand stealthily removing one of the gilded buttons of his chuba. Fortunately he managed to move faster than the thief! He caught the man and held him until the police arrived. The Maharaja himself did not take such a great delight in racing and only came along with us once, but Chuni and I found it great fun and very relaxing after each week's hectic round of engagements.

The royal party also included a number of children, notably Their Highnesses's young son, the Crown Prince Jigme, who was then only seven but was able to play with his future wife, Ashi Kesang, the daughter of Tobgye and Chuni. Many years later, in 1949, Ashi Kesang came to England to study at the House of Citizenship. She was the first Bhutanese to visit Europe and to cross an ocean. She also visited the United

States. She married the Crown Prince of Bhutan in 1951. He succeeded to the throne in the following year. The other children ranged in age from five to seventeen, and we were able to take them on some of our outings. The young ones particularly enjoyed trips in the launch that Sir John Anderson kindly put at our disposal. In the evenings, the little girls could be seen peeping through the banisters at 42 Chowringhee to see what the grown-ups were wearing.

Sometimes, in the evenings, when formality could be relaxed, we went to the cinema. This was particularly popular with the royal party, though it was not always easy to arrange the necessary block-bookings for forty people if the film we wanted to see was a popular one.

On one occasion Samdup came up and confidentially asked me: 'Memsahib, did you know that the Maharani asked to be excused from her dinner engagement last night, saying she was sick?'

'Yes, Samdup, I know,' I replied. 'What of it?'

'Well, Memsahib, I'm sorry to say that she was not sick at all but went to see the film which you have booked seats for this evening.'

Fortunately I was able to cancel the booking and instead get hold of seats for an equally entertaining film that no one had yet seen. The Maharani never realized the trouble she had caused!

Everyone in Calcutta treated Their Highnesses with the greatest kindness and, as the visit progressed, it became apparent that we had been able to provide return hospitality for only a fraction of those who had entertained them. We therefore decided that the best way to resolve the dilemma would be to throw an enormous cocktail party at 42 Chowringhee and invite everyone we had not been able to invite individually. I arranged for Firpo's to provide the food and Pinjo also lent a hand. The Bhutanese retainers, meanwhile, were put to work stringing fairy lights around the garden and building a massive bonfire in the centre of the lawn to counteract the evening chill.

The cocktail party was a resounding success. People wearing conventional European evening dress mingled with the brightly clad Bhutanese and Sikkimese, and were served by Sikkimese chaprassys in red coats trimmed with black and bamboo hats decked with peacock feathers. Several of the Bhutanese men were excellent dancers, so entertainment was provided too. Everyone enjoyed themselves and the event was pronounced the party of the season.

When the visit to Calcutta came to an end, the Royal party went on a pilgrimage to Benares and Bodh Gaya, although Derrick and I excused ourselves from this part of the tour – indeed Derrick had to go straight into hospital to have his tonsils out!

The Maharani went by herself to Nepal as a private pilgrim, while the Maharaja came up to Gangtok and spent five days as our guest at the Residency, when he took great pains to express to Derrick his gratitude for all the kindness that had been shown him during his visit. He finally said goodbye to us on 18 February 1935.

ONE MORNING SOON AFTER we had returned to the less hectic routine of life at the Residency, Derrick came out of his study carrying a batch of papers in his hand.

'I've just been doing my accounts—and do you know what?' he said, flourishing the papers, which were covered with scribbled calculations. 'It seems to cost me no more being married than it did when I was single.'

'Well, of course, I brought everything out with me, didn't I?' I replied; 'except a wedding dress.'

Derrick sat down and did not say anything. For a moment he looked away abstractedly as though slightly worried, then he turned back to me. 'I've often wondered how you managed to get out here from England,' he said.

'Well, I came on borrowed money,' I confessed. 'But it was borrowed money on a certainty.'

'What certainty?' he asked sharply.

'Well, whatever Aunt Mary did for my sister, Aunt Maggie

always did the same for me. I know that Mary got £500 in Aunt Mary's will, so I will get £500 from Aunt Maggie. On the strength of that, I borrowed £250 from Mary to come out here.'

Derrick stood up abruptly. 'Well, I'm not having a wife on borrowed money,' he declared firmly, and there and then he wrote out a cheque for £250 and gave it to me. 'Send that to your sister first thing in the morning!'

14 'The Service Always Comes First'

FROM THE START of January 1935, Derrick's attention was focused upon Lhasa. With the departure in the November of the preceding year of Huang Mu-sung, the leader of the Chinese Mission of Condolence, the crisis in The Holy City had relaxed enough for everybody to take stock and consider counter moves. The British view then was that, despite initial fears that the new Tibetan Government might not be able to stand up to concerted Chinese pressure, it had come through pretty well. Whatever face-saving fictions the Chinese might be putting about, the Tibetans had not acceded to Huang's principal demands.

On 20 January, 1935, Derrick wrote a long letter to Sir Aubrey Metcalfe, the Foreign Secretary of the Government of India, outlining what he thought should be done. His main suggestion was that he be sent again to Lhasa in order to consolidate Rai Bahadur Norbhu's good work and clearly demonstrate to the Tibetans that the British Government retained a very strong interest in their affairs. He also asked that ample funds to the tune of some 70,000 rupees be granted him so that he could be appropriately lavish. 'A visit to Lhasa is seriously prejudiced if the Political Officer cannot cut a bit of a figure,' he argued; also there was a need for a 'disguised subsidy', in order to give the Tibetans some concrete token of British support. He proposed in addition to be allowed to offer the Tibetans exemption for three years on instalments due on munitions supplies and to be able to offer further supplies of munitions if they were wanted. He also suggested military training should be provided, at British expense. As regards the Chinese, his suggestion was that their officials currently in Lhasa be regarded as foreigners and Tibet treated, according to established practice, as autonomous. He strongly felt too that, should a permanent Chinese representation emerge in Lhasa, then this should be matched by a similar British presence, as had been the wish of the late Dalai Lama.

The letter was a spirited argument for wholehearted British support of Tibetan autonomy. The visit it proposed would have an altogether different complexion from the one that we made to Lhasa in 1933. That had been an essentially social affair; the proposed forthcoming one, on the other hand, would be a full-scale official visit with funding and a mandate sufficient to make it an effective counterpoise to the Chinese Mission of Condolence.

During the early part of 1935 the vexed matter of the return of the exiled Panchen Lama also seemed to be coming to a head. In 1934, there had of course been disturbing reports that he was now supported by 'some thousands of troops' and might be planning to return to Tibet by force. Closer enquiries, however, tended to suggest that his much reported military capability did not really amount to very much; perhaps a hundred or two ill-trained men and no more than a thousand German rifles purchased in Shanghai.

One day in early January, two representatives of the Panchen Lama called on Derrick in Gangtok on their way to Lhasa from India. They brought with them an old letter of instructions dated February 1933 in which the Panchen Lama had set out for the benefit of the Dalai Lama (who had then been alive) the terms on which he was prepared to return to Tibet, which were:

> restoration of all property belonging to Tashilhunpo, control of Shigatse and two other dzongs, restoration of all property confiscated from Tashilhunpo officials and their servants, and freedom of movement for them throughout Tibet, refund of all sums collected

in Tsang province under the new tax laws, the Tashilhunpo administration to be independent, the Tibetan Government to refrain from levying any military or civil taxes in Tsang Province.

The death of the Dalai Lama had meant that no formal reply to this letter had ever been sent. The two representatives were now briefed to secure the return of the Panchen Lama with the minimum of delay once these terms had been established 'as decisively as a knife cuts flesh'. On 17 January the Panchen Lama himself informed Derrick that he had sent his representatives to negotiate with the Tibetan Government 'so that I can return without having recourse to arms'. He added that upon his return to Tibet he hoped Anglo-Tibetan friendship might be placed upon an even firmer footing and indicated that, in the event of negotiations running into difficulties, he would appreciate any help that the British Government might be able to give, or at least, if we could not be actively helpful, that we would remain neutral.

By the time he had received this letter, Derrick had already telegraphed the Kashag and the Panchen Lama's representatives, who were by then in Lhasa, advising both parties to concentrate upon obtaining a workable settlement. In February, however, reports reached British ears via the Peking Embassy that negotiations were encountering obstacles over the division of the spheres to be controlled by the Panchen and Dalai Lamas respectively. Accordingly, the Foreign Department telegraphed Derrick on 21 April 1935, authorizing him to advise the Panchen Lama to moderate his demands and be satisfied if the Tibetan Government would agree to allow him to enjoy the position and possessions that had been his before his flight into exile.

In March 1935 there were rumours that the Chinese were threatening the Tibetans with war if Huang's terms were not accepted and, in the following month, that the followers of the Panchen Lama were in a similarly bellicose mood. Then in May the news was that the Panchen Lama was actually travelling towards Tibet and that he had sent to Shigatse for three hundred men to escort him over the border. These developments only served to strengthen Derrick's arguments that he be sent to Lhasa that year and, in due course, London and Delhi moved round to his way of thinking.

On the matter of providing the Tibetans with military assistance in the event of Chinese attack, the British view was quite adamant, there could be none.

Derrick was therefore directed to accept an invitation to go to Lhasa if one was received from the Regent; if one was not received, on the other hand, he could ask to be invited himself. In the event, the Reting Rinpoché did express a wish for Derrick to come to Lhasa but did not want to appear to be the initiating party for fear of antagonizing anti-British elements. He therefore suggested that Derrick telegraph him so that, effectively, he did not have to accept responsibility for the visit.

At this point Derrick was at the heart of great events and there was the opportunity for him to have a decisive hand in shaping developments that would have a profound effect on Tibet and the whole Himalayan region for many years to come. Tragically, however, fate now dealt him a severe blow.

Dr. Hendricks, our GP at Gangtok, a most conscientious doctor, insisted that Derrick and I have regular check-ups. In 1935, not long after the latest of these, Hendricks paid an unexpected call upon the Residency. He asked to see Derrick and the two of them went into Derrick's private office and closed the door. They were closeted together for some time. Finally, Dr. Hendricks came out and asked to have a word with me. With grave face Dr. Hendricks told me that Derrick had uraemia, a condition resulting from the failure of the kidneys to eliminate toxins from the blood and that there was no known treatment.

Dr. Hendricks advised against the journey to Tibet. However, even though we now knew that he was very ill, Derrick insisted on going on the visit to Lhasa, it being of vital importance at such a sensitive time. Derrick's position was that there could be no debate about it. He had to go. The service always comes first. I did not try to stand in Derrick's way as far as going to Lhasa was concerned. I too understood the needs of the service and it would never have occurred to me to try to deflect him from any course of action that he felt to be his duty.

Looking back, I cannot say that I recall Derrick acting in an unusual way at this time. He may have been a little silent and preoccupied, but he was not one to spend much time brooding, so he must have set his own feelings aside and thrown himself into his work, particularly his preparations for Lhasa, which had now assumed a new and special urgency.

One piece of good news also arrived in 1935, Derrick heard that he had been awarded the CIE, the Companion of the Most Eminent Order of the Indian Empire, in the Birthday Honours List. This was an indication that the work he was doing in the service was appreciated. He could have received the insignia in India from the Viceroy, but when he saw Lord Willingdon in private he asked whether the investiture could be put off until we returned to England so that he could receive the insignia from the King. Lord Willingdon graciously agreed to this request.

A letter arrived for Derrick from the Regent at the end of May, informing him that in June or July he intended to visit the neighbourhood of the Chokhorgyal monastery, which was about four days' journey south-east of Lhasa, to make enquiries in connection with the anticipated new incarnation of the Dalai Lama. In view of his unavoidable absence from Lhasa, the Regent requested Derrick to delay his arrival there until August. A highly charged matter like the reincarnation of the Dalai Lama spawned all manner of fanciful rumours. The bazaars were abuzz with them. One, said to have orig-inated in Gyantse, told of a miraculous birth: a child issuing from its mother's arm pit. Derrick surmised that the Regent was investigating this. As it turned out the Regent's mission to Chokhorgyal had a different, but no less strange, object.

15   The Last Long Journey

WE CONTINUED TO make preparations for the long journey from Gangtok to Lhasa which in the event was to be the last journey Derrick and I would make together. We set off on 13 June 1935, putting behind us for the time being our un-voiced anxieties about Derrick's health. That year we were accompanied by Rai Bahadur Norbhu, Samdup and his wife, Pinjo, four clerks and about forty servants. Our transport consisted of over a hundred animals—yaks, *dzos*, donkeys and ponies.

Heavy rain had washed away the track in places and we ourselves experienced a few torrential downpours, but at last we ascended through a splendour of rhododendrons towards the Natu-la. There was a little snow on the slopes surrounding the pass itself, which we crossed in a mist. Then we descended to Yatung, where we stayed for over three weeks. Despite a few disquieting earthquake tremors, our stay here was as pleasant as in preceding years. Rai Sahib Dr. Tonyot Tsering Kazi, the sub-assistant surgeon at the Agency, and the clerks, put on a theatrical piece for us, an Indian play called *The Drama of the Life of the Buddha*.

At Yatung we received more news of the Regent's mys-terious journey to the neighbourhood of Chokhorgyal mon-astery. The Geshe Rinpoché of Drongkar monastery in the Upper Chumbi Valley told Derrick that there was a lake named Lhamo Lhatso in the vicinity of the monastery that possessed oracular properties. In order to find the new incarnation of the Dalai Lama, lamas would perform a special ceremony on the banks of the lake over which the Regent would preside. Afterwards a view of the particular village in which the birth would take place would miraculously appear in the waters, along with other significant signs.

In Yatung Derrick also received confirmation that the grand tomb of the Thirteenth Dalai Lama was now complete and that an official ceremony had been performed there on 13 June by Trimön Shapé.

At Kangbu, on the way to Phari, we experienced the luxury of hot spring baths. There were seventeen sulphur springs here, with temperatures ranging from 104° to 117° F, some of them enclosed by small shelters, We were actually accommodated in one of these: a simple stone affair with a turf roof, whitewashed walls and curtained windows. The bath itself was in the centre of the main room; it had a shingle bottom and the ceiling was open to the sky. There was a second bathroom adjacent; also a place for our beds, a small sewing room and finally an area where we could sit and take our meals.

I retain a particularly vivid recollection of toiling across the Tuna Plain a few days later. It seemed to stretch on endlessly. In fact, crossing it was regarded as so arduous a task that it had been dubbed 'Elephant Weeping Plain' or, alternatively, 'Three Sisters Plain', after three sisters who had set out to cross it but who had, one by one, dropped dead during the journey, not one of them reaching the other side! We did not even have the consolation of seeing the glorious peak of Chomolhari as all but the lower portions of the mountains were obscured by clouds.

We reached Gyantse on 20 July and there met the new British Trade Agent, Captain Keith Battye, who had gone to a great deal of trouble to see that everything was comfortable for us at the dak bungalow. Another new arrival was Captain James Guthrie, a young Scottish doctor, just out of medical school, doing his first tour of duty as Agency Surgeon. Nevertheless, he had some serious cases to deal with, like the young girl who had been mauled by a bear at Tashilhunpo and had to have her arm amputated.

During a pleasant stay in Gyantse we renewed our acquaintance with many old Tibetan friends. There was the Taring Raja and his son Chime, Kyipup and Dorje Phagmo, whom we went to visit again at Samding, taking a small clockwork toy for her young nephew. This little present went down very well, and the august lady and her family later came over to Gyantse to watch the firework display that we were again putting on at the Agency. Unfortunately, this display was not the pyrotechnic extravaganza it was intended to be—but we had a very happy dinner afterwards and then some late-night Tibetan dancing.

Derrick's health continued to be variable. There were days when he felt fine and we allowed ourselves the luxury of hoping that all would be well, but there were also days when the situation was reversed and then our hopes were broken. For instance, we were watching a game of polo being played one day and Derrick decided he'd love to have a game himself. He was out there with them the next time they played and had a marvellous time, but the following day he was completely exhausted. That was typical of the way his illness took him.

Our party left Gyantse on 6 August, Captain Guthrie coming along with us as medical officer, assisted by Rai Sahib Bo. We made our first camp at Gobshi, then travelled on to Ralung in heavy rain and camped in a quagmire. In the afternoon a spate of water completely washed away the road just as the last stragglers of our transport were coming up. They eventually got in after some delay and hasty revetment operations; they had been held up by the near deaths of three donkeys along the trail.

Derrick felt rather weak that day but Rai Sahib Bo changed his medicine, which did seem to make him feel much stronger. We travelled slowly up to the 16,600 foot Karo-la, from where we enjoyed a magnificent view of snowclad hills and glaciers. Our camp that night was by the river at Dzara. Derrick went to bed before dinner, feeling unwell.

It was raw and cold next morning, having snowed during the night, though this soon turned to sleet and rain. The

Yamdrok Tso and the Damo Tso looked cold and bleak when they at last swung into view later in the morning.

Despite a rainy start, the next day's march (10 August), was the most beautiful of all. The surrounding hills looked gloriously green, dappled here and there with patches of red where the underlying clay showed through and with occasional vivid patches of mustard. The ground around us was enamelled with delphiniums, forget-me-nots and other wild flowers. We camped at Pede that day and in the morning set out for Kampa Partse by way of the 15,400 foot Kampa-la, over which Derrick had to be carried in the dandy that we had brought along on Dr. Hendricks' advice. That was the only time he had to use it.

A terrific storm got up after we had got into camp at Kongka Dzong on the following day. It rained heavily and thundered until well into the night, and at this inauspicious moment a happy but entirely unexpected event took place.

I had noticed at dinner that Samdup was looking rather worried, so I asked him what was the matter.

'She's gone and done it!' he exclaimed in his quaint English.

'Done what, Samdup?' I asked.

He then explained to me that his wife, Phagmo, a handsome girl from the Chumbi Valley, had given birth to a baby daughter. That was the first I knew of her condition!

'I must come and see at once,' I said.

So, despite the torrential rain, I hurried with Samdup to the little bell tent where we found Phagmo sitting on a pile of bodens with Samdup's greatcoat slung around her shoulders, trying to feed the new arrival. The tent was leaking and most of the space inside was taken up with packing cases; nevertheless, even in these difficult conditions, Phagmo had managed to deliver herself of a fine child with dark hair and scarcely a wrinkle on its little face.

BEFORE WE LEFT GYANTSE, news had come through that negotiations between the Tibetan Government and the

(Previous page) Image in the Jokhang.

The monk proctors at Drepung, with their staffs of office.

(Opposite) Ganden Monastery.

The Towa Dzongpön and his wife.

Samye Monastery.

Derrick in the Kangbu hot springs.

Tsetang ferry.

Rowing down the Tsangpo.

Derrick filming on the Yab La.

The Regent.

Lunch at Bondong Shapé's house with Battye and Guthrie.

Dorji Phagmo with her sister, nephew and his son.

Mrs Bumthang and self at Tsetang.

Chörten at Samye.

Main Lhakang at Ganden.

Panchen Lama's representatives had reached an advanced stage. The chief remaining stumbling-block was apparently the question of Shigatse Dzong; the Panchen Lama was prepared to concede that the Lhasa Government might collect revenues in the area but he wanted to retain the right to appoint the dzongpön himself. Agreement, however, might not be far off, and, according to Mr. Pande, a Nepalese official, the Tibetan Government were only awaiting Derrick's arrival in Lhasa before reaching a final decision.

These reports did not, however, spur us on to Lhasa post-haste for, although our invitation was for mid-August, it was understood that the Regent was still away with a great search-party looking for the new incarnation of the Dalai Lama and in the circumstances it was considered best not to arrive in the holy city much before he did. We therefore took our time and travelled by an indirect but much more interesting route, down the great Tsangpo river. We got into coracles and went for a three-day cruise downstream.

Our boatmen were cheery fellows who spoke some sort of local dialect that Derrick could not understand. They sang a great deal as they went about their work or whistled through their teeth, took snuff and heartily regaled themselves from time to time with tsampa and chang. They also brought sheep with them: a thing that I could not understand, until Derrick explained.

'Once they've got downstream there'll be no chance whatsoever of sailing back up here. The current is far too strong for that. They'll hoist their coracles onto their backs and carry them back along the banks of the river. They bring the sheep along to act as pack-animals and carry their other possessions.'

The first day of our little cruise was by far the most adventurous as well as the most exhausting, for we covered a total of thirty-five miles. At first we coasted along merrily enough, passing various small riverside villages and an imposing gompa surmounting a rocky pinnacle. Then we noticed that there was water slurping around our feet.

'Oh Derrick—we're leaking!' I cried.

Derrick at once leapt up and drew the boatman's attention to the situation. The fellow was as cool as a cucumber. In a leisurely sort of way, he splashed around until he had located the leak, then he picked up my cape, which was lying nearby—it was made of a Tibetan woollen material called *thigmo*—and, without so much as a by-your-leave, ripped a piece out of it and used it as a makeshift patch. I was frankly amazed—but it did seem to do the trick!

Towards lunch-time, we decided that it would be nice to go ashore to eat, but the boatman warned us against this, saying that there were quicksands in the vicinity. A stiff head wind got up and our rate of progress was slowed to an almost imperceptible crawl. It took us two hours to cover six miles to a great triangular rock that jutted imposingly out of the water and we were by then passing through some of the most forbidding country that I'd ever seen. There were desolate dunes all along the northern bank of the river and winds had blown the sand right up into the ravines of the rocky hills that we could see further back. To the south there were just great barren mountains.

A little way beyond the great rock, the wind really started to blow and to whip up the water. The river was about three quarters of a mile wide at this point and moving rather sluggishly. We therefore tried to manoeuvre across to the other side, where the current seemed to be flowing more strongly. Half way there, however, the water became very choppy and the coracle was buffetted about alarmingly. We all felt so uneasy when this happened that we began to undo our mackintoshes, anticipating that we might have to swim for it.

However, after our boatmen had exerted truly Trojan efforts to get us across, we found that we could not land as there were quicksands all along the bank!

'Nothing for it but to push on,' Derrick said.

Fortunately, the wind now dropped and the river became calmer again, though time was passing and daylight was failing fast. We passed around more brandy and pressed on into the thickening gloom. Long before we had reached our camping place, night overtook us, and then the moon rose, 'a white and shapeless mass,'

> −like a dying lady, lean and pale,
> That totters forth wrap't in a gauzy veil,
> Out of her chamber, led by the insane
> and feeble wanderings of her fading brain ...

It was a great relief, when about 8 p.m. we eventually heard voices in that darkness and then saw lights−one, two, finally three−which meant that our campsite was near by. Afterwards the other boats came in, one by one. None of their occupants, however, reported the great storm that we had encountered. Why had we been singled out? I wondered−and then I remembered the warning that the Dalai Lama had given to us in 1933 not to sail down the river again!

Two days later we arrived at Tsetang, where we visited some fine monasteries. We asked about the legend of the first field of barley in Tibet which was said to be near by. Two things were known about this mythical field: that its crop had to be donated to the Dalai Lama and that if any other field in Tibet failed to bear barley then a handful of soil from this particular field scattered over it would render it fertile again. After Tsetang, we crossed the river again and soon arrived at Samyé, where we found Captain Battye awaiting us, having come up from Gyantse.

Samyé monastery is remarkable. It dates from the eighth century and is reputed to be the oldest Buddhist monastery in Tibet. Its origins are connected with Guru Rinpoché, also known as Padmasambhava. Samyé is also said to be built in accordance with a mandala-like structure of the world. At its centre is Mount Meru, at its corners four great continents and around the edge an outer boundary wall of iron mountains. Samyé too had an outer boundary wall, though not of iron mountains. Instead there were thousands of chörtens built on top of an oval masonry wall. Inside, a central temple, built in the Chinese style, the symbol of Mount Meru, dominated the monastery. There were smaller buildings at each of the cardinal points and four enormous chörtens, each painted a symbolic colour, red for fire, green for water, white for good and black for evil. We could also see a massive wall inside the compound where huge thangkas were hung on special occasions.

We were formally met at the entrance and conducted around by the three dzongpöns and Shasur Depön, a lay official who was in charge of the renovation work. He put in a request to Derrick for facilities to purchase gold in India, this being needed, among other things, for regilding the roofs.

At the entrance to one of the chapels was a fine old bronze bell bearing an inscription to King Trisong Detsen (741-798) by one of his queens. The interior of every storey of the temple was in a different style; the ground floor Chinese, the second floor Tibetan and the top floor Indian. There were beautiful images in each, including ones of the seven most holy Buddhas and the Seven Medicine Buddhas, some of them studded with turquoises, pieces of amber and what seemed to be fragments of dark blue glass. We were shown rooms where the Dalai Lamas stayed when paying official visits; they seemed surprisingly small. We next passed down a covered alleyway where there were eight hundred and sixty prayer-wheels, some of which we turned as we passed. To my consternation, as I spun one it fell to the ground with a great clatter.

'I suppose I've no luck left!' I said as I picked it up.

In another *lhakang* (chapel) we saw images of the local oracles and, below, the three twenty-five foot swords that guard the room where the breath of everyone who dies anywhere in the world is said to pass. There was no question of seeing this cell as it had been firmly locked and sealed by the present oracle.

The Shasur Depön entertained us to tea at his house shortly afterwards. His wife and children joined us. The

children had been at the children's party I had organized in
Lhasa in 1933. We then proceeded on our indirect journey to
Lhasa, our next objective being the monastery of Ganden,
one of the three great monasteries of the Lhasa region. In
order to reach Ganden we headed north from the Tsangpo
Valley across the Gokar-la (17,000 ft.), through beautiful
country that reminded us of parts of Bhutan, on account of
its lovely flowers: delphiniums, clematis, aconites, asters,
vetches and several bluish-purple flowers I didn't recognize.
There were no trees, however, only scrub. On the third day
we reached Dechen Dzong in the valley of the Kyi Chu,
where the transport was changed, and where we were greeted
by the monk who had been deputed to guide us in Lhasa.

From then on the track seemed to merge with the river for
long stretches and at one point we passed some wonderful
images carved upon the wayside rocks; also strange holes
formed by the habit of Buddhist travellers of grinding pebbles
when passing. One of our mules which had gone on ahead
had been sickly for a while and it gave up the ghost. When
our main party reached it the carcass was a seething mass of
voracious vultures. There were so many of them that the path
was blocked and others, for whom there was no room at the
feast, hovered near by with grim expectancy.

On our way to our campsite at Shatra-hog, which was
situated in a walled garden, we passed several caravans. The
largest of these, which was owned by some Chinese traders
who wore very wide-brimmed hats, comprised a hundred
and twenty mules carrying tea and scarves. The other caravans
had about fifty mules apiece.

The next day we visited the great monastery of Ganden,
spread panoramically across the upper portions of a curved
hillside rather like an amphitheatre. Although it appeared to
be just as large as Drepung it housed only about 3,300 monks,
allocated between two colleges. It too had golden roofs that
shone with burnished brilliance in the morning sunshine.

We were greeted by officials and ushered to a room
above the main assembly hall for tea and rice. Eggs

and butter were presented to us. Then we were conducted to see the resting place of Tsongkhapa (1357-1419), the great monastic reformer who founded the Gelugpa school of Tibetan Buddhism to which the line of the Dalai Lamas belongs. He founded Ganden in 1409 and taught, meditated, wrote and organized the monastic community there. His remains now rested in a magnificent gold and silver chörten encrusted with turquoise, onyx, amber, coral and other semi-precious stones. A statue of Tsongkhapa stood before it, with silver water-bowls and flowers clustered around its base.

We then passed into a hall in which two hundred young monks were receiving teachings. Masses of butter lamps were burning, reminding me of the great annual festival of Nga Chö Chenmo which falls on the twenty-fifth day of the tenth month of the Tibetan year, celebrating the anniversary of Tsongkhapa's birth. In the main assembly hall, said to be capable of accommodating the monastery's entire population, the smell of rancid butter was quite overpowering and the floors were treacherously slippery. It was a good thing we had our guides and torches to light the way.

Later our party broke up and we were separately shown individual monks' rooms. The one we visited was a neat and tidy little cell, with a boden where the occupant could sit to meditate and study sacred texts. After lunch, Derrick gave the monastery 1,000 rupees, courtesy of the Government of India. The money was received by the *shengos* (proctors) with much bowing of boarded shoulders and display of large red tongues.

Lhasa now lay two days' march to the south-east, but, even though it was so close, we didn't quicken our pace. On the first day out of Ganden, we paused at mid-morning for tea and to read our mail, which had caught up with us. When we got to camp at Dechen just before noon, we could see the Iron Hill of Chakpori, the Medical College of Lhasa, away in the distance.

As we approached Lhasa the next day, I began to experience

strong but mixed feelings of anticipation. Worried as I was
about Derrick's uncertain health, I was yet keenly looking
forward to meeting old friends again, like Jigme and Mary-la
Taring. But what of the changes that had taken place since the
passing of His Holiness? Kunphel-la was banished, Lungshar
lay eyeless in a dungeon, and a number of other high officials
had gone. Then there were the Chinese. What effect would
their renewed presence have had on the holy city?

16 The Holy City Again

LHASA AGAIN! As soon as we had been ferried across the river we saw big WELCOME notices and crowds of eager, curious people who jostled the members of our party. There were officials too, and, a little further down the road Jigme Taring, spruce and handsome as ever, had a guard of honour drawn up for us. Derrick inspected the soldiers who wore khaki uniforms and Wolesley helmets. Afterwards the soldiers 'formed fours' to march back to Lhasa. Unfortunately, the road was in places completely submerged under pools of water, so they had to break ranks and proceed individually along walls and banks to drier ground. In a splendid reception ten more officials were waiting to offer us katas, tea and rice, but our pleasure was marred by the presence of the Chinese wireless operator and five Chinese soldiers.

Later we rode into the bazaar, then on past the hovels where the *ragyapa* lived. The ragyapa were an outcast section of Tibetan society who lived by performing services that Tibetans in general didn't want to do, like butchering animals or cutting up corpses for the traditional 'sky burial'. We then crossed the Yutok Bridge and proceeded on past the Potala and Chakpori.

Rampa, our lay guide, was waiting to greet us when we arrived at Dekyi Lingka, our home for the next eleven weeks, and at once offered us an excellent meal provided by the Tibetan Government. After eating, we set about rearranging all the furniture to our liking. Not all our party could be accommodated in the house this year, so Captain Battye and some of the others pitched tents for themselves out among the willows.

Repeating the pattern of 1933, our first few weeks were largely occupied with the social round, although this time we did not have an initial three day settling in period and the stream of callers began immediately.

The Regent and Trimön Shapé we did not see right away as on our second day a letter arrived saying they would not be returning from the quest for the next Dalai Lama for another four or five weeks. But we did meet the remaining members of the Kashag on the first day, when they came to Dekyi Lingka with presents of sheep, rice, flour, butter and eggs. They were even more friendly than two years ago. Later I was delighted to see Jigme and Mary-la and to find that they hadn't changed at all, except that Mary-la didn't look too well. She told me that since we'd last seen each other she'd had a baby daughter: a big, bonny girl whom they had nicknamed 'Peggy' after me!

The Chikyap Khenpo, head of all the monks, came to see us on the second day, along with the Panchen Lama's representative. Then on the third day, Derrick, Battye and Guthrie donned full uniform to pay an official call on the Lönchen. The meeting took place in one of the chambers of the Potala, everyone being seated on low bodens upon the floor. The Lönchen greeted them most cordially and Derrick felt that he seemed altogether better disposed than in 1933. He still retained his old tendency to put on airs and graces though.

And so it went on, calling and being called upon, for many days. What struck me most strongly was how genuinely pleased everyone was to see us again; we were treated like long-lost friends. Clearly, the people of Lhasa had been under some strain since the death of His Holiness and fear of the Chinese loomed large in everybody's consciousness; I think our presence gave some sense of support.

Our relations with the Chinese contingent in Lhasa were on an entirely different footing. We found them more or less outcasts in Lhasa. We ourselves could not avoid having social dealings with them, however, and while all the necessary formalities were observed, underneath lurked a deep undercurrent of mutual suspicion.

Mr. William Tsiang, the principal Chinese representative, who had preceded Huang Mu-sung to Lhasa, was a thin man with slicked-back hair and a small moustache. He favoured Western dress: suits, bow-ties—and he was often seen in Lhasa sporting a black bowler hat. He was a small man and tended to hold his head down and to peer at the world through thick glasses. Mr. Chang, his wireless operator, on the other hand, was a toothy and loquacious man, who displayed his nervous temperament by talking and grinning continually. Both these gentlemen were a source of merriment to our party.

On 7 September, we had the dubious pleasure of lunching with them at their house in Lhasa. Having drunk innumerable cups of perfumed tea, we were escorted into the dining-room, where a truly vast lunch had been prepared for us. It amounted to some twenty-eight courses in all, which were listed on the menus with which we were presented; Chinese characters on the left and roughly typed English equivalents on the right. Unfortunately my pleasure in this banquet was marred by two things.

Firstly, I was absolutely convinced that Mr. Tsiang and his minions were conspiring in the most sinister Fu Manchu style to poison Derrick. I therefore paid rather more attention to what was going on at the periphery than to the meal itself. I watched the servants closely for signs of anything suspicious; and I watched Mr. Tsiang too, in case he should try to pass any of them a secret signal. Of course it would have been highly discourteous of me not to have eaten at all, so I sampled all the dishes with my chopsticks, but only took a little of each.

The second thing that spoiled the Chinese banquet for me was the fact that there were four spitoons in the room, one strategically sited in each of the four corners, and our host

204 Memoirs of a Political Officer's Wife

made liberal use of them throughout the more than two and a half hours we were seated at his table. In all fairness, I have to admit he was a pretty good shot. As far as I could tell he did not miss once.

Alcohol flowed freely, including the popular *crème de menthe*. The insipid Mr. Chang was pouring a glass of this for Dr. Bo when a large piece of paper came out of the bottle and fell into the glass. Mr. Chang did not hesitate: he removed the offending item with his fingers, hurled it vehemently into a corner, and went on pouring as if nothing had happened.

Möndö, apparently not at all hindered by his monastic vows, proved himself adept at reducing the whisky supply. I feared that Mr. Tsiang might disapprove of this, especially when I overheard him referring to our friend as a 'monkey'. Upon reflection, however, I realized that he probably meant 'monk'. It really was quite fortunate that Mr. Tsiang's linguistic eccentricities did not lead to quite serious misunderstandings.

After this feast we adjourned to the other room for more tea. Mr. Tsiang then thrust a plate before me that seemed to contain a mass of tiny splinters.

'These are American products that we always use after lunch,' he informed me, and proceeded to give a graphic demonstration of how one picks one's teeth. I did not follow his example but I did take one toothpick out of courtesy and put it in my pocket. After taking our leave, we laughed all the way back to Dekyi Lingka, though this was probably as much from relief as from amusement at the eccentricities of our hosts.

Later Keith Battye reported an amusing conversation that had been overheard between two monks in Lhasa at about this time. It went as follows:

First Monk: 'It would appear that the members of the British Mission are of infinitely higher standing than those of the Chinese Mission.'

Second Monk:'I agree. Did you notice how the Chinese

Mission arrived in Lhasa in dandies, while the British Mission rode in on horses and relegated their only dandy to a dog?'

First Monk: 'Yes, and this also: that whereas the Chinese officials all eat, work and sleep in one room each, the British Lönchen Sahib [Derrick] has an office, the Am-chhi Sahib [Dr. Guthrie] has a hospital and even the Lhacham Kusho [myself] has an office, while they all eat together in a special dining room and I understand never quarrel at meals!'

NOT LONG AFTER OUR ARRIVAL in Lhasa, the party season got into full swing and we soon found ourselves caught up in this merry round of conviviality. In addition to the other parties and entertainments going on at this time, we ourselves sponsored a three-day Ache Lhamo performance with the help of the new Dronyer Chempo (Chamberlain), who had at one time been Tibetan Trade Agent in Gyantse. The site selected was in a spacious lingka beside the Kyi Chu where a convenient house stood on one side of a large open space. All high officials, monastic and lay, were invited, the latter bringing their gorgeously dressed wives along with them. They were accommodated in tents pitched on two sides of the open space, while tents for our party, the Kashag and for third and fourth rank officials were erected at the end of the house. From here we could obtain a good view of the performances, which took place in an open-sided pavilion in the centre, and also of the other spectators. The vast kitchens and dining-rooms, which played a vital part in the event, were in the house itself. Masses of ordinary people also turned up and on the last day we estimated that the crowd must number ten thousand.

The theatrical troupes were changed each day; the most popular was a bawdy company of some twenty men and two girls who danced magnificently. The loudest laugh went up on the third day when a handsome Tibetan youth dressed in women's clothing was helped through the final stages of pregnancy by a midwife and, after a brief struggle was finally delivered of a small blue cushion. The 'baby' was then carried around the arena in the arms of a male 'nurse' to the general hilarity of the onlookers. A couple of minutes later, the 'mother', apparently none the worse for her confinement, was capering round with the other artistes in a highly strenuous dance.

At the end of each day's performance, katas and presents were distributed to the artistes, then there was a 'flour throwing' ceremony and finally a shower of meteor-like katas weighted with coins streamed through the air towards the arena from all directions as a token of general appreciation. We provided an additional bonus at the end of the second day's proceedings in the form of a firework display.

The Ache Lhamo was a great success – except for the Chinese contingent who were visibly put out that things had gone off so much to our credit.

Once again we gave many cinema shows. In addition to some favourite Charlie Chaplins, we showed films of our 1933 tour and tried a little mild propaganda with films of King George V's Silver Jubilee Celebrations and of the Hendon Air Display, as well as others of educational value. Of course, another popular event we could not omit repeating was the children's party.

By 1935, Ringang was well advanced with his scheme for bringing electricity to Lhasa. The current was conducted over a distance of about four miles by high tension cable from the power house beyond Trapchi to a sub-station in the city situated just below Ringang's own house. His brother had a rather bigger house just across the street, which had been converted into a theatre complete with dress circle, boxes and gallery. The 'stalls' were occupied by a number of horses. A temporary connection was put in here so that a cinema show could be given which we were invited to attend.

We also took advantage of the period spent waiting for the return of the Regent to do a large amount of sightseeing. We went to Trapchi again, and also to the Potala, where the centre of attraction was now the sumptuous new tomb of the late Dalai Lama. Quantities of gold as well as other precious metals and *objets d'art* had been lavished on it, being the contents of the late Dalai Lama's treasury augmented by generous gifts from the Chinese. There were also two galleries, each about twelve feet from the other, from which the tomb could be viewed from all angles. New images of the late Dalai Lama could also be seen at Drepung and some of the other monasteries that we visited.

Unusually, for a time we were not the only Western visitor in Lhasa. In early October two American travellers turned up, Suydam Cutting and Arthur Vernay. They were the first Americans ever to visit Lhasa and spent about ten days sightseeing.

Inevitably, living at the altitude at which Lhasa is situated for a fairly long period of time, tempers occasionally became frayed and there were periods when relations between our party came under stress. Captains Battye and Guthrie enjoyed themselves well enough in Lhasa during the initial weeks. As time wore on, however, and the Regent still failed to return, Battye in particular began to grow restless. He was frustrated at being unable to smoke in public or go hunting. He did, however, find some compensation in tending a wounded lammergeier that he found with a wing torn.

Guthrie, who was then a young medical officer of twenty-eight had been in the Indian Medical Service for only about four years. The conditions under which he had to work were very primitive. Before he could begin operating in his makeshift theatre, he had first to send a man up onto the roof to scare away the sparrows whose droppings, falling through the open skylight, would otherwise have fouled the operating theatre. He had to ensure that all fires in the adjacent rooms had been extinguished, so that he could have a reasonably smoke-free atmosphere in which to work. Finally, he had to try to keep the room free of spectators and often had to mount a guard on the door to ensure that casual visitors did not enter. Understandably, Guthrie was unwilling to undertake major surgery and restricted himself to extracting teeth and sewing up wounds and torn ears. He did, however, remove two supernumary thumbs, stitch up the severed trachea of an attempted suicide and remove a massive six pound tumour from a woman's back. Since the death of the Dalai Lama a ban hitherto imposed upon wearing spectacles in public had been lifted and a number of officials presented themselves at the hospital to have their eyes tested for glasses.

Occasionally our forays out of Dekyi Lingka took us into the town of Lhasa and its lively bazaar. I was never entirely alone—when Derrick couldn't come he insisted I took four servants with me. As a European woman I was inevitably the object of much curiosity. On one such visit I made a bad name for myself, if only temporarily. For visits to holy places I invariably wore a long skirt so as not to offend monastic sensibilities but now, on our return from one such visit, I was riding side-saddle. The Tibetans noticed my flesh-coloured stockings and, with much hilarity, dubbed me 'the naked lady'.

But our life in Lhasa had a more serious side to it. We had set off from Gyantse before Derrick received his final instructions. These were formulated in London by the Secretary of State for India and were relayed to us via the Governement of India. They caught up with us while we were on the road to Lhasa and ran broadly as follows:

Derrick was to broach orally the matter of the Panchen Lama's return and seek to promote a settlement without involving HM Government or the Government of India with any responsibilities for its maintenance. He was also to investigate the effects of the Huang Mu-sung mission and in particular to ascertain whether Willilam Tsiang could be regarded as a permanent Chinese representative in Lhasa. If he was, then Derrick was to find out what the Tibetan Government's attitude would be to similar British representation. No commitment was to be made on this count, however; ideally HM Government would like to see the status quo continued: viz. no permanent Chinese or British representation in Lhasa. If by chance the Tibetans raised the question of active British assistance in the event of Chinese aggression, Derrick was to reply that the Chinese were not expected to pursue such a policy at present, but that if they did threaten to do so then HM Government would attempt to persuade them against it by diplomatic means. Additional requests for further supplies of munitions, military training and suchlike were to be referred back to the Government of India. In addition, the Tibetan Government were to be assured that HM Government was anxious to maintain its traditional friendly relationship with the Tibetan people and to deal directly with their government; also that it recognized the de facto autonomy of Tibet within the theoretical suzerainty of China. Among other assurances, Derrick was to impress upon the Tibetan Government that HM Government would not have any dealings with the Government of China over its head.

Those first few weeks in Lhasa before official meetings got under way in earnest were a useful time for Derrick to find out what changes had taken place in political life since our last visit and where power and influence now effectively lay. That the death of a strong-minded ruler like the late Dalai Lama should have caused great changes he fully anticipated, but not perhaps to the extent that he found to be the case. The Regent, though broadly faithful to his predecessor's policies, simply was not the same political force in the land that His Holiness had been. He tended to lean on the Kashag, who in turn seemed to be afraid of doing anything without first consulting the National Assembly. The Assembly, which consisted of about a hundred commoners split up into various factions, in its turn had to consider the way things were blowing in the great monasteries and among the general public. In short, the old order had been virtually turned upon its head. Having taken stock of this, Derrick acted accordingly and on this visit was careful to extend the range of his social visits.

Of the Kashag, Trimön Shapé continued to be the dominant force he had been during His Holiness's time. His views tended to be shared by Bhondong Shapé, a new appointee in his mid-forties and the second in influence in the Kashag. The views of the only monk, the Kalon Lama, tended to carry weight, as did those of Tendong Shapé, an army Depön (Colonel) in his early fifties, but Langchungna Shapé enjoyed little influence and tended to follow where he was led.

In recent times attempts had been made to bring Tsarong Dzasa back into the Kashag but for reasons of his own he had resisted such promotion. He was, however, back in Lhasa again and was certainly still the first gentleman of Tibet. He was popular with monks and laity alike, and also had the ear of the Regent.

The Lönchen, on the other hand, was decidedly not a force to be reckoned with and remained as ineffectual as he had been in 1933. Of the other prominent Tibetans, our friends Yutok Depön and Jigme Taring, both also strongly pro-British, were influential, as was Dingcha Kusho, formerly the Chief of Police in Lhasa, now senior Dzongpön at Shigatse. In fact, pro-British feeling was running high in Lhasa, which was quite understandable in view of the prevalent Chinese threat.

Derrick, accompanied by Battye, paid his first formal call upon the Shapés in the Kashag offices at the Jokhang on 26 September, four weeks after our arrival. Present were Bhondong Shapé, Tendong Shapé, Langchungna Shapé and the Kalön Lama; Ringang sat in as interpreter. After a few sips of tea, discussions started, punctuated by everybody helping themselves to the raisins and other sweets which had been placed in the centre of the table. The meeting broke up after about an hour and a half, and then I joined Derrick and the others at the Lönchen's house for lunch, followed by a photographic session.

Among the matters that came up at that meeting with the Kashag was the question of the Panchen Lama. Although the news which had reached Derrick on his way up to Lhasa had caused him to become optimistic that agreement might be close, when he finally got there he found that his hopes had

been misplaced. The Tibetan Government would not accede
to the Panchen Lama's terms and still held out on several
important points. As neither side was prepared to give way,
the situation had reached deadlock. The Kashag now wanted
Derrick to use his influence with the Panchen Lama to try to
get him to modify his terms still further.

Underlying this issue lay the Tibetans' fear of Chinese
aggression. Derrick found this uppermost in everyone's mind
in Lhasa. It had inspired the Tibetans with a new appreciation
of the value of friendship with the British Government, and
this was continually emphasized to Derrick, in both formal
and informal meetings with officials. Derrick, in his turn,
could assure them that his own government also valued the
relationship and wanted to see it continue.

A matter that he also found disquieting and possibly
indicative of a slight weakening of Tibetan resolve was the
fact that a murder committed by the Chinese contingent in
Lhasa had as yet gone unpunished, although subsequently
the National Assembly did declare the culprits guilty and
fined them a total of £11.

As regards the matter of permanent British representation
in Lhasa, the Tibetans were quite clear on that point: they did
not want it. But neither did they want permanent Chinese
representation. As for Mr. Tsiang and his colleagues, they
had no prestige, were not liked and were regarded at most as
a temporary imposition. The Tibetans had twice telegraphed
Nanking, requesting their recall, but had received no reply.
They had also requested the British Government not to grant
visas to new personnel being sent out from China to relieve
the existing ones.

Derrick's efforts to assure the Tibetans that the British
were reliable and trustworthy friends could easily have been
undermined when a rather unexpected and embarrassing task
landed on his desk in Lhasa. His old friend, Frank Kingdon
Ward, the famous plant-hunter, was travelling in south-
eastern Tibet that year in search of botanical specimens and
he had deliberately strayed well beyond the limits set out in

his permit. This greatly annoyed the Tibetan Government.

'They're even saying that if British travellers can't be trusted they might withdraw permission for the Mount Everest Expedition planned for next year,' Derrick said.

With much effort and skilful diplomacy, he managed to smooth things over, and Kingdon Ward was able to continue his plant-hunting activities in blissful ignorance of the trouble he'd caused.

Despite being generally pro-British, the overall political climate in 1935 was distinctly conservative. Things had changed in this respect and there was now very little concern with improving Tibet's own military capability or with pushing on with the late Dalai Lama's modernization programme.

But even if his instructions prevented him from giving the Tibetans the kind of assurances of support they wanted, Derrick nevertheless did all in his power to make them aware that the British were seriously concerned and would do everything that they could short of military intervention to help them. He also urged his superiors to take a firm diplomatic line in their negotiations with the Chinese and to register a formal protest against their sending troops and officials back with the Panchen Lama, should he return. The British Government accepted his arguments and representations being made to Nanking were extended to include this point.

Later history was in fact to show that the Tibetans did hold firm, despite no assurances of British military support. They did not back down on their resistance to the idea of Chinese troops and soldiers returning with the Panchen Lama, and they later refused to recognize Chinese suzerainty either in theory or in fact. Thus their resolve was, if anything, strengthened, and Derrick was no doubt at least partially responsible for this. His presence in Lhasa at this critical time and his knowledge of Tibetan politics, which was undoubtedly far greater than that of any of his predecessors, enabled him to talk personally to all the influential officials and give them

moral support. As B.J. Gould, Derrick's successor as PO
Sikkim, wrote in the following year:

> The presence of Mr. Williamson in Lhasa personified
> His Majesty's Government's policy of support of
> the Tibetan Government and at the same time made
> it possible to avoid the complications which might
> have been incidental to any attempt to state in
> writing the qualified assurances which he was
> authorized to give.

17 Tragedy in the Garden of Happiness

TOWARDS THE END of October, after we had been in Lhasa for about two months, we heard to our great pleasure that the Regent was returning to the capital. Samdup went out to watch him arrive and was able to take some excellent film of the event from vantage points we could not have reached. The Regent's name was Thubten Jamphel Yeshe Tempar Gyantsen and he was born of poor parents in Takpo province, about eight or ten days' journey south-east of Lhasa. He was a child novice at Sera until he was old enough to read, after which he was taken to Reting monastery, where he was regarded as the local tulku. By a process of divination conducted by the Shapés and the National Assembly, he had become Regent.

Derrick and Battye went to call on him on 23 October. On his return Derrick told me how friendly the Regent had been. The new incarnation of the Dalai Lama had not yet been discovered but some very clear indications were received in Lhamo Lhatso, the lake near the Chokhorgyal monastery. Apparently the Regent had seen three Tibetan letters. Ah, Ka, and Ma, then a great monastery with jade and gold roofs. A road ran past the monastery and on to a house standing at the foot of a hill. This house also had some turquoise tiles on its roof, and a brown and white spotted dog guarding its courtyard. The Regent was confident that after such clear indications he would be able to find the child next year. The Regent's optimism was not misplaced. The signs he received at Lhamo Lhatso did lead his search parties to the house in the small farming village of Takster, just east of Kumbum in eastern Tibet, where the Fourteenth Dalai Lama was discovered in 1937.

Trimön Shapé also returned to Lhasa with the Regent and we met him at about the same time. On the first meeting I was disturbed by his appearance. He seemed at least ten years older than when we had seen him two years before, and very solemn.

The Regent broke with custom to leave his house and come to watch our second firework display, held near Dekyi Lingka. In keeping with the dignity of his office, he did not mix with the crowd but watched from a distance. It made a spectacular show over the river. He also enjoyed the film show that we mounted for him a few days later at his own house. Tsarong and the Regent's Dzasa were there too. On that occasion we were able to photograph the Regent. Later he asked to see our dogs. I complied with this request and sent them all along, including the seven little apsos I'd bought for various people, but I put my foot down firmly and insisted they all be returned and not enveigled away as presents.

Captain Guthrie was able to find out more about the Regent than any of us because he was asked to give him a medical examination, not an easy thing to do as he was wearing so many robes and accessories. When all these had been removed and investigations conducted, Guthrie found that there wasn't anything fundamentally amiss with the Regent's health, though his hollow chest, his anaemia and the generally poor condition of his malnourished body would make him easy prey to infection.

Meanwhile, Derrick, despite the fact that he was often far from fit, continued his unceasing efforts to arrange some sort of accommodation between the Tibetan Government and the exiled Panchen Lama. By mid-October only three points remained at issue: the control of the army in Tsang province, the control of a few districts that had not hitherto fallen within the Panchen Lama's ambit, and of course the matter of his bringing Chinese troops and officials back to Tibet with him. The Tibetan Government used the Chinese wireless to inform the Lama, who was then in Kumbum, of the state of play and they took it as a cue for optimism when they received no reply. Derrick was not so optimistic, however, and he got in touch with the Lama himself to point out that only three points in his demands remained to which the Tibetan Government could not give assent. In his reply, the Lama emphasized strongly that the Tibetan Government's contention that he wished to bring Chinese troops and officials back to Tibet with him was untrue: 'This is not one of the points of my demands.'

Whatever the Lama's own wishes, it was by then quite clear that the Chinese had definite views on the matter. They had informed the Tibetan Government that they intended sending an escort back with the Panchen Lama and even went so far as to be specific as to numbers: viz three hundred soldiers and ten officials. The Tibetan Government informed them that this was not permissible.

This matter came up at one of the final official meetings Derrick had in Lhasa. Fear of the Chinese was again high at that point.

The Tibetans pressed Derrick to refer the matter to his government, saying that if we could not try 'one really strong bluff', then they would be forced to throw in their hand.

Derrick felt that the Tibetans' fears of the Chinese were largely unfounded but genuine for all that. He therefore telegraphed back to his superior officer, urging that 'we should do everything that may be possible to help the Tibetan Government and to convince them that they have not merely our mild diplomatic backing but our strong support.' He added that he would be grateful to receive orders as to the reply to be given to the Tibetan Government as soon as possible as he planned to leave Lhasa in the first week of November at the latest.

But Derrick could neither carry his work further, nor leave

Lhasa. In the early part of November his health began to deteriorate rapidly. At first it was just a matter of his having to drop out of some engagements; then he had to take to his bed for whole days. We never discussed his health, but I was very worried. I did my best to look after him and to carry on. That was really all I could do. The Tibetans were all most kind. A stream of visitors called at Dekyi Lingka as the news got around, enquiring after Derrick's health and bringing presents. Even Mr. Tsiang called.

The situation was made especially critical by the fact that Lhasa was so remote and far from modern medical facilities. Captain Guthrie and Rai Sahib Bo did their best, but I wanted Dr. Hendricks, our own GP from Gangtok, to be there, so I telegraphed for him to come up. I received a reply that he was on his way.

Captain Battye also rose to the occasion. He took over all Derrick's official duties, which included the negotiations over the return of the Panchen Lama. These were never brought to a successful conclusion, for the exiled Lama, who had for so long been a kind of political football in Central Asian politics, passed away in Jyekundo in December 1937, just a stone's throw away from the homeland which he was never to see again.

Battye telegraphed India for an aeroplane to be sent in so that Derrick could be treated in a hospital in Calcutta, and then went off to prospect for a landing site. He found a suitable one out near Sera monastery. Then the disappointing news reached us that a Royal Air Force plane, while it might land easily enough, would have no chance of taking off again at a height of 12,000 feet. It simply was not technically possible in those days. Nevertheless, Battye still went along to the Kashag and tried to get them to grant formal permission.

The shapés, he informed me on his return, were all most anxious to do what they could, but were unfortunately and reluctantly obliged to withhold permission on the grounds that if they gave it they would also have to agree to an air service between Lhasa and China, which they had been recently resisting.

'That doesn't sound very convincing,' I protested. 'I mean – this is a matter of life and death!'

'I know, that's what I told them. I think there's a deeper reason there. The monks at Sera might revolt if an aeroplane landed near their monastery. They would at least stone the machine and any guards posted round it.'

I longed for Dr. Hendricks to arrive. Derrick was now permanently in his bed upstairs at Dekyi Lingka. He had bad nights and during the day frequently became delirious and violent. On 14 November he became a little quieter, however, and ate a little better. He stayed awake for most of that day, listening to the gramophone. It seemed to soothe him.

Perhaps at that moment I dared to believe there might be hope, but all such prospects were dashed on the night of 15 November, which was a very troubled one for him. The next day he was quiet but seemed to have slipped completely into a coma. He was very weak by then and suffered from bad hiccoughs, but he did manage to take food.

Derrick did not sleep the next night until the early hours of the following morning, despite having been given a vapour bath and morphia and bromide. As the first faint light of the new day began to filter through the glassless windows at Dekyi Lingka, I could see that his face had assumed an ominous ashen colour. Guthrie came in to examine him and found his pulse very weak. By now Derrick couldn't eat as he was unable to swallow. We wired Dr. Hendricks, who must have reached Phari by now.

We gave Derrick another vapour bath in bed before lunch that day – 17 November – but afterwards he seemed to relapse completely into coma. I was sitting at his bedside in a daze partly brought on by anxiety, partly through lack of sleep. I hadn't had my clothes off or lain down for several days. Guthrie had also given me some kind of sedative to steady me.

At about 5.25 pm, Derrick suddenly sank and his face became ashen again. Then, without warning, he raised himself, threw his arms around me and gave me a big hug. After that he lay back and in a moment was gone. Captain Guthrie tried artificial respiration and heart massage—but all to no avail.

A huge emptiness seemed to fill that small Tibetan room and to spread out from it to the four quarters.

18 'Far Away Yet Among Friends'

DERRICK LOOKED SO happy and peaceful lying in his bed at Dekyi Lingka on the morning of 18 November. I could not believe he was no longer with us.

I busied myself packing and generally making preparations for leaving. That took my mind off things. Many kind Tibetan friends also came to call and offer their condolences, including Jigme and Mary-la. I could see that they fully shared my grief. Their kindness was touching and very supportive. Mary stayed with me that night. I also received numerous telegrams of condolence.

Our servants were all very distressed at Derrick's passing, particularly poor Samdup, who had been with him for twelve years and in that time had formed a deep bond of attachment. After Derrick had been placed in his coffin later that day, they all went and filed past, paying their last respects.

Meanwhile Battye and Norbhu had official matters in hand and were presenting our formal farewells to the Regent, the Lönchen and the Kashag.

The next day I answered telegrams and received various callers, including Mr. and Mrs. Tsarong and Ringang, who had become special friends. Meeting them in such circumstances brought fully to light the depth of relationship that had developed between us. Then sadly our melancholy cavalcade wound its way out of the holy city under a lovely cloudless sky. There were all the usual honours and formalities to observe but afterwards we were alone on the stony road southwards. Derrick's coffin was carried ahead of us and his pony, led fully saddled but riderless, with the stirrups turned.

At Gyantse, Captain Salomons, the new CO took me to see the place in the cemetery that had been selected for Derrick's grave. It was a pleasant spot in a nice sunny position. There were also more telegrams and I read them while Derrick's body was taken away to the civil hospital for a post mortem.

The funeral was held on the morning of 25 November. Tibetan officials presented me with katas; then the officers and troops of the escort arrived and laid green fir wreaths on Derrick's coffin as it lay in the dak bungalow. Afterwards we left in slow procession for the cemetery, the firing party leading, then the buglers, the body and bearers, the chief mourners and finally the civilian mourners. Troops lined the route. I took Bruce with me.

Keith Battye read the burial service. After the first part, the Union Jack, the wreaths and other items were removed from the coffin before it was slowly lowered into the ground. Then, after the second part of the service, three volleys were fired into the air and the buglers sounded the Last Post—always very haunting, but never more so than up there in that remote outpost on the Roof of the World. The men all stood to attention and the officers saluted; then reveille was sounded. Finally, the firing party moved off, followed by the rest of us.

I later received a kind letter from Tobgye and another very helpful one from Dr. Graham. I also heard the news that the new PO Sikkim was to be B.J. (later Sir Basil) Gould. He stepped off the ship in Bombay to be informed of his new appointment, a fitting one for he had served in Tibet as a British Trade Agent for about a year and a half back in 1911. He and I had bereavement in common: he had only lately lost his wife in Quetta in tragic circumstances.

I paid a final visit to Derrick's grave with Samdup before setting off from Gyantse with Battye and Salomons escorting me. In bitterly cold weather we crossed the Tuna Plain encountering fierce dust storms as we rode. At Yatung all Derrick's dear friends — Tonyot, Sangye and all the clerks — came out and I had the painful business of having to say last farewells to them. Here, Salomons left us but Battye accompanied me through the peaceful pine forests and on up to the Natu-la, where there was snow and the going was slippery, but we were rewarded with a magnificent view from the top. Chomolhari in particular stood out in all its snow-mantled grandeur.

As we approached Gangtok, His Highness the Maharaja kindly sent a dandy and two cars to bring me in, and we were met all along the way by friends and well-wishers. At the empty Residency I found Dr. and Mrs. Hendricks waiting for me. I had, of course, telegraphed news of Derrick's death south to Dr. Hendricks. On receiving it at Gyantse, he had turned around and returned home. Then Mrs. Dudley came and many of the local people, and finally His Highness himself, who presented his condolences in his own gentle and dignified way. When everyone had gone, the Residency echoed with a particular emptiness and desolation.

Fortunately, Betty Clarke came over from Darjeeling and proved to be a great comfort and help. I don't know if I could have borne it without her. Joan Townend also came up from Calcutta. Helped by servants that our kind Bhutanese friends had put at our disposal, I packed up all my possessions so that they could be shipped home to England.

ON MY WAY HOME, I passed through Calcutta, where I was received by Lord Willingdon, the Viceroy, and Lady Willingdon. In a moving ceremony in which full recognition was paid to Derrick's many talents, virtues and achievements, his CIE was presented to me.

'Normally this honour should be returned upon the death of the recipient,' Lord Willingdon told me. 'But in this case, it has been deemed appropriate that you keep it in perpetuity.'

I called also on the Head of the Indian Medical Service to

tell him that I hoped in future steps would be taken to ensure that no young wife again found herself in the position in which I had found myself in Lhasa.

'In your husband's case, there could have been no other outcome,' he informed me. 'It was just a matter of time. Had he remained at sea level, he might have extended his life for a few months more, but I've no doubt he went as he would have wanted to go: doing the work he loved among the people he loved.'

And so, still only twenty-nine but now a widow I returned to England. Both the Williamsons and my own family offered me homes but, having tasted what it was like to have my own, I felt I could not go back to living with other people again. Instead I bought myself a former vicarage in Cheshire and set up house there for myself, with all the mementos of my life with Derrick.

The two and a half years that I spent with him were the happiest and richest of my whole life. In a sense that brief period was my life. Nothing that went before or has happened since came up to their pitch. Naturally, I felt at the time that it was very hard that our life together should be cut short so soon, but now I'm convinced that things in life work out as they're meant to. Indeed, if I were to be offered the chance of living that all too brief period over again, I would do so without a moment's hesitation—even if I knew at the same time what the final outcome would be.

Bronze memorial plaque.

Derrick's grave at Gyantse.

(Following page) The Potala reflected in flood water.

Chomolhari from near Dochen.

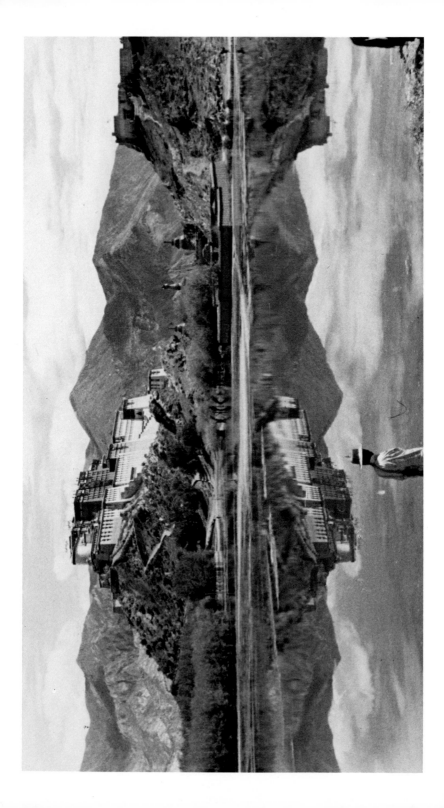

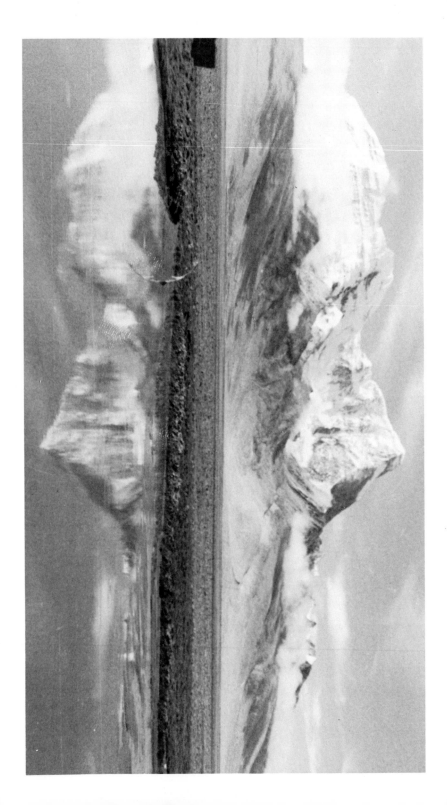

*The following four pages feature examples of
a large selection of artefacts collected by
Mr. and Mrs. Williamson and eventually presented
to the Cambridge University Museum of
Archaeology and Anthropology.*

Portable shrine from Tibet.

(Opposite) Silver mounted cup, gift of the Prince of Torgut.

Bhutanese sword, shield, helmet and beer container.

Bhutanese teapot.

A wall plaque, Chenrezig, dorje and bell, symbols and prayer wheel.

Epilogue

In 1937 I took out to Derrick's grave in Gyantse a simple granite cross and slab that I had had made in Aberdeen. There on the bustling quayside at Bombay was Samdup, waiting to offer his services. I was delighted to see him and together we crossed India on the luxurious Blue Train. Then it was on up toward the hills by the old familiar route. When we arrived back in Gangtok, it was like coming home again, so little had changed.

There were, of course, many joyful reunions there. Tobgye and Chuni, Dr. and Mrs. Hendricks, the Dudleys—it was so good to see them all again. There were our old retainers too, including Pinjo, who had now been elevated to the rank of Royal Cook. Before I'd left Gyantse the time before, I'd heard that it would be likely that Pinjo would be out of job, for the new PO Sikkim, B.J. Gould, was bringing his own Indian cook up with him. I'd known for a long time before that the Maharaja was secretly using Pinjo to cook for him whenever he had an important dinner, so before leaving I'd gone along to the Palace and left word there that, if desired, Pinjo was available for permanent employment. The Maharaja had eagerly engaged him, and Pinjo seemed to be doing very well. Pinjo, bless him, cooked enough bread for the whole of my stay in Gangtok.

The new Political Officer, B.J. Gould was reluctant to allow me to go on to Tibet with Derrick's memorial stone. He told me he had made a ruling that no European woman could go there unless accompanied by a European man. I wondered if that applied to people who had permission directly from the Government of India. B.J. was surprised to hear I had this permission – which indeed I had obtained before I left in 1935.

'In any case,' I told him, 'Samdup will be with me and three of Tobgye's men: two syces and a muleteer. I'm also taking a Sherpa cook, a sweeper and one extra muleteer, who will accompany me as far as Yatung. I shall be perfectly discreet. When I sign the visitors' book in the dak bungalow I shall put 'M.D. Williamson'. Nobody will know whether that person is a man or a woman!' B.J. reluctantly gave way.

And so, once more, I found myself climbing towards the Natu-la and from there descending into the wooded Chumbi Valley and on by the familiar route onto the fascinating table-land of Tibet. At every stopping place, old and friendly faces came out to greet me; everywhere there were poignant reminders of my life with Derrick. It seemed strange to sit at camp in the evening and not to be able to turn and see him there again, his pipe in his mouth, making notes or writing his reports.

The business of erecting the cross on Derrick's grave was already under way when I arrived but the base was yet to come. I therefore engaged Rai Sahib Wangdi and one of the Agency clerks to finish the work. When complete the new fixtures were a simple yet dignified memorial and I was confident that the grave would be cared for. The inscription on the slab read, 'Far Away Yet Among Friends', a fitting epitaph. The Tibetans – and indeed all the peoples of these regions, the Sikkimese and the Bhutanese as well – *were* our friends. They loved and respected Derrick and he never felt so happy as when he was among them.

Years later, in 1954, devastating floods in Gyantse damaged the Agency, completely destroying the staff quarters and killing several of the occupants. The cemetery was washed away and not only Derrick's grave went but those of all the 1904 Younghusband people as well.

But Derrick did have another memorial that was to last.

Back in Gangtok, His Highness the Maharaja had commissioned a new maternity wing for the local hospital. This was duly named after Derrick and bore a bronze plaque with his portrait, name, dates and motto: *Aude et Prevalebis* (Dare and You Will Succeed). I was asked to officiate at the opening ceremony.

'I know that it would have been his wish that if there were to be a memorial it should be something to help others,' I told the assembled gathering; then I cut a green ribbon and opened the door of the new wing with a golden key.

Appendix: The Williamson Collection in the Cambridge University Museum of Archaeology and Anthropology

In 1972 Mrs. Margaret D. Williamson presented 155 artefacts from Tibet and the neighbouring countries of Sikkim and Bhutan to Emmanuel College, Cambridge, in memory of her late husband Frederick Williamson, CIE, ICS, a former member of the College. The items have been placed by the College on deposit at the University Museum of Archaeology and Anthropology (registration numbers 1976.D.1 – 155). Seven further items were added to the gift and deposited in 1985 (numbers 1985.D.1 – 7). Selected items from the collection are on public display at the Museum from time to time: other specimens may be examined there by researchers through prior appointment.

The Williamson specimens add greatly to the quality and range of the Museum's holdings from Tibet, Bhutan and Sikkim. The collection includes items of outstanding interest and quality: their importance is enhanced by the detail of some recorded provenances and by the fact that some were gifts to the Williamsons from such as the Thirteenth Dalai Lama and the Maharaja of Bhutan.

Here it is appropriate to give only an indication of the range of items in the Williamson collection. The most numerous specimens are receptacles such as bowls, teapots, and incense burners, often of copper or brass but including examples made from or decorated with wood, jade, ivory, silver and gold: several have their monastic provenances recorded. There are temple trumpets, drums and bells, an altar piece, a prayer wheel and images of the Buddha.

Weapons include swords, daggers, bows and arrows as well as archery targets and a shield. By contrast the collection also contains baskets, a table, snuff-bottle, chopsticks, ladles and spoons. There are three book-covers and a printing block. Clothing and textiles include a variety of hats, rugs, ceremonial scarves and a large ceremonial tent.

Outstanding items include:

1976.D.99 Portable shrine
1976.D.69 Silver mounted cup
1976.D.80 Bhutanese royal sword

In 1985 Mrs. Williamson made a generous and substantial gift to Cambridge University for the establishment of a Frederick Williamson Memorial Fund. The income of the Fund may be expended by its Board of Managers, appointed by the University, for 'furthering research relating to the peoples of Tibet, Bhutan, Sikkim, and neighbouring Himalayan areas, their society, religion and material culture; and for the development of the Williamson Collection in the Museum of Archaeology and Anthropology.' The Museum and University have thus been given, not only a wholly exceptional collection of artefacts from Tibet and neighbouring countries, but also the facility to augment the collection as opportunity arises and to support research in these areas.

David W. Phillipson
Curator
1987

Index

Bruce, 61, 74, 89, 95, 116
Buddha of compassion,
  Chenrezi, 83, 119
Buddhas, 120, 162, 196
Buddhism, brought to Tibet, 19,
  119, prevalence of religious
  observance in Tibet, 19,
  doctrine of reincarnation, 20,
  emphasis on sanctity of life,
  84, 120, evidence of faith in
  Lhasa. 111, monastic training,
  122, Drugpa school, 15,
  Gelugpa tradition, 159, 198,
  Sakya order, 147
Bumthang, 67, 75–7, 137
Butter Festival, 112

Cabra ferry, 89
Calcutta, 49, 175–80
Campbell, Major W.L., 38
Chaknak monastery, 132
Chakpori, 93, 102, 198, 201
Chaksam, 89
Champithang, 64
Chand, Faquir, 170
Chang, Mr., 203, 204
Changlochen, Kusho, 91, 95,
  110
Chang-na-na, 70
Chang Tang, 18
Changu Lake, 62
Chenrezig, 83, 119
Chense Lingka, 123, 126, 144
Chikyap Khenpo, the, 124, 202
Chi Lai pass, 70
Children's parties, 117–18, 197
Chin, Shu-zen, 44, 46
China, relations with Tibet,
  1910 invasion, 23, 107,
  expulsion, 1912, 23, 107,
  Tibetan wish for

independence from China, 23,
  China encourages rivalry
  between Panchen and Dalai
  Lamas, 24, 159, Dalai Lama's
  foreign policy towards China,
  97–8, Chinese Mission of
  Condolence, 130, 162, 165,
  166, 169, 183, 184, 208,
  Advance Party, 163–4, 165,
  166, 171, increased tension,
  169–73, offensive behaviour,
  171–2, fourteen articles
  devised, 172, British role
  unacceptable to Chinese, 173,
  departure of Huang Mu-
  sung, 173, 183, rumours of
  threat of war, 185–6,
  presence in Lhasa, 201–5,
  fear of Chinese, 202, 211, 217,
  representation in Lhasa,
  208–9, Tibetan resistance
  holds firm, 212, continued
  Chinese intention to bring in
  troops, 217
Chinese banquet, 203
Chinese Turkestan, 41–7
Chögyal, 54
Chokhorgyal monastery, 187,
  215
Chomolhari, 63, 167
Chumbi river, 64, 65
Chumbi Valley, 12, 14, 61, 82,
  189, 192, 226
Chusul, 89–90
Cinema shows, 72, 104, 117,
  118, 206
Circumambulation, 111, 119
Clarke, Betty, 223
Cossipore, 177
Curzon, Lord, 22
Cutting, Sudyam, 42, 207

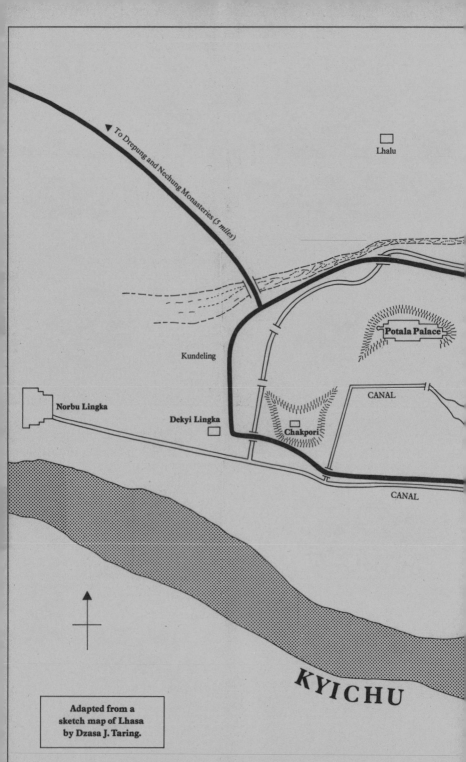

To Drepung and Nechung Monasteries (5 miles)

Lhalu

Kundeling

Potala Palace

Norbu Lingka

Dekyi Lingka

Chakpori

CANAL

CANAL

KYICHU

Adapted from a
sketch map of Lhasa
by Dzasa J. Taring.

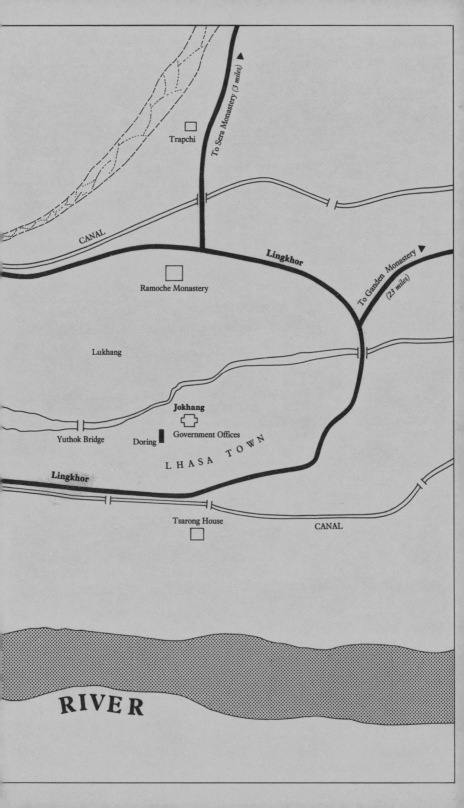